Structuralism and the Biblical Text

Religion and Reason 32

Method and Theory
in the Study and Interpretation of Religion

Mouton Publishers · Berlin · New York · Amsterdam

Structuralism
and the Biblical Text

DAVID GREENWOOD
University of Maryland

Mouton Publishers · Berlin · New York · Amsterdam

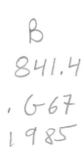

B
841.4
. G67
1985

Library of Congress Cataloging in Publication Data

Greenwood, David, 1927–1984.
  Structuralism and the biblical text.
  (Religion and reason ; 32)
  Bibliography: p.
  Includes index.
  1. Structuralism–History. 2. Bible–Criticism, interpretation,
etc.–History–20th century. I. Title. II. Series.
B841.4.G67 1985   220.6'01   85-11424
  ISBN 0-89925-103-X (U.S.)

CIP-Kurztitelaufnahme der Deutschen Bibliothek

Greenwood, David:
Structuralism and the biblical text / David Greenwood. – Berlin ;
New York ; Amsterdam : Mouton, 1985.
    (Religion and reason ; 32)
    ISBN 3-11-010336-2
NE GT

Printed on acid free paper

Contents

"ineffable individuality" of the text — primary symbolization — Freud's concept of the Prohibition — the
personal voice — proairetic code — semic code —
cultural code — hermeneutic code — symbolic code —
methodology of *S/Z* — Grunkel's approach to the story
of Jacob and the angel — unstructured equilibrium and
language systems — the linguistic "mark" — Propp's
"functions" — asyndetic structuring — metonymic logic —
language and the subjectivity of the author.

4. THE METHODOLOGY OF A. J. GREIMAS   63

Semantique structurale and *Du sens* — the opposition
between "immanence" and "manifestation" — the
semantic representation of a lexeme — sememes —
classemes — isotopies of a text — normalization —
the six roles of actants or nominal groups — the actantial
model — logomachic character of texts — reduction of
texts to series of sememes — global meaning —
descriptive algorithms — Jean Calloud's analysis of
Matthew 4:1-11 — the "signified" of the text —
actantial positions of Jesus and Satan in the temptation
story — semiotics of manipulation.

5. THE METHODOLOGY OF ERHART GÜTTEMANNS   75

Generative poetics — text and *Gattung* — eight axioms
underlying generative poetics — textual actuality —
differentiation of texts by genres — transformations —
narrative mode in the gospels — base-grammar of
narrative — transformational grammar — dialectical
mediation — narrative competence of *homo
loquens* — Guttgemanns' criticisms of New Testament
theology — theology as a science — the place of faith —
the 47 methodological rules of generative poetics —
definition of *kerygma* — influence of Chomsky's
Syntactic Structures — the value of generative poetics —
the place of inspiration.

Preface

The application of structuralist methods of analysis to the text of the Holy Bible started in the early 1960's with the work of Sir Edmund Leach. He used a structuralist methodology which owed a certain amount to that which Claude Lévi-Strauss had employed in his *Anthropologie Structurale* of 1958. In September 1969 almost two hundred biblical scholars, including Roland Barthes, convened at Chantilly under the auspices of the *Association Catholique Française pour l'Etude · de la Bible* to discuss the relationship between structuralism and the biblical text. In 1970 Erhardt Güttgemanns of the University of Bonn founded the journal *Linguistica Biblica* to promulgate the structuralist views of himself and others. In February 1971 Roland Barthes and Jean Starobinski introduced structuralist analysis of the biblical text to a colloquium of Protestant scholars at the University of Geneva. In 1973 the Toronto Semiotic Circle was founded by structuralist scholars of the University of Toronto, and has subsequently exerted considerable influence, especially through the periodic meetings of the International Institute for Semiotic and Structural Studies.

It is impossible to predict how long the use of structuralist methods will continue. It is often said in the mid-1980's that the age is post-structuralist, and that the shortcomings of structuralism are now so generally admitted as to preclude any foreseeable future for the movement. It should be remembered, however, that structuralism is an interdisciplinary enterprise, involving principles drawn from anthropology, hermeneutics, linguistics, literary criticism, communication theory, and several other academic subjects. In a broad sense linguistic structuralism is a branch of – and to some scholars largely conterminous with – semiotics, and nobody at present is willing to presage the early demise of that science. Structuralist thinking of one kind or another is likely

to continue for some time, though its character and boundaries are hardly likely to remain fixed or permanent. One would hope that its present rather unsatisfactory terminology may also be improved.

This work is primarily intended for scholars and others who may need a general survey of structuralist procedures and methodologies as they have been applied to the biblical text. Among those to whose assistance and advice I am most indebted are the Oriel Professor of the Interpretation of Holy Scripture at Oxford, Dr. Ernest Nicholson, Dr. Fitzroy Pyle of the University of Dublin, Professor Amos Wilder of the Harvard Divinity School and Dr. Joseph Zalotay of the Catholic University of America in Washington, D.C. I should add that many of the books referred to in the notes and the Select Bibliography have been issued in similar editions on both sides of the Atlantic. I have indicated the edition or editions that I was using: a particular citation is not as a rule intended to indicate any special preference.

D.G.
University of Maryland
College Park, Maryland.
23 May 1984

Foreword

Structuralism, first developed in the fields of linguistics and anthropology, was soon applied to and adopted by a variety of other disciplines. Among them was biblical studies. At first, biblical structuralism was practiced by non-biblicists. Then, gradually, the more literarily inclined biblical scholars tried their hand at it, so that by the 1970's there was a growing bibliography, and structuralism began to take its place among the sub-groupings of biblical studies.

But to many biblical scholars, untrained in literary methodologies, structuralist analysis and exegesis remained alien. Biblicists had little understanding of or sympathy for its approach or goals. To make matters worse, biblical structuralists themselves did not always seem to agree on what to do or how to do it; and at times their relationship to more "traditional" forms of structuralism seemed, at best, distant.

The present volume is designed to alleviate this confusion and present a coherent discussion of structuralism as it has been applied to the biblical text. In this major synthesis, David Greenwood explains the origin and development of biblical structuralism, and devotes a section to each of its most prominent practicioners. The explication is lucid, sensitive, and objective; advances are praised and deficiencies are criticized, and all in language easily understood by non-structuralists. Thus this book can serve as an introduction to biblical structuralism as well as a reference for those already initiated into this area.

David Greenwood was, in many ways, the perfect author for such a book. The holder of a Ph.D. in English Literature from the University of Dublin and a Doctor of Sacred Theology from the Catholic University of America, he was Associate Professor of Comparative Literature at the University of Maryland, where he taught courses on Bible and Literature for many years. His

publications, in English, French, and Latin, also give proof to his expertise in these two areas and his interest in their interrelation. To our great sadness and regret, Professor Greenwood did not live to see the publication of this book. He died suddenly on May 26, 1984. But the scholarly contribution that he makes here will live on for many years.

Adele Berlin
Associate Professor of Hebrew
University of Maryland

1

Structuralist Procedures in General

The roots of structuralism are to be found principally in the linguistic theories of Ferdinand de Saussure. His posthumous *Cours de Linguistique Générale* was reconstructed principally from the notes of two of his former students, Charles Bally and Albert Sechehaye, at the University of Geneva, and published in 1915, two years after his death. It soon became accepted as an authoritative work in linguistics, and established a number of fundamental principles which are inherent in linguistic and structuralist methodologies at the present day. Among these, perhaps the most important is the concept of the linguistic sign as an entity consisting of a signifier and a signified which are bound together in a complex, functional relationship. It would be hard to overemphasize the influence that this notion subsequently exerted: the treatment of the signifier independently of the signified permitted the development of modern scientific phonemics which, especially in the hands of such members of the Prague Circle as Nikolay Troubetzkoy and Roman Jakobson, has been one of the outstanding methodological successes of structuralism.

On the other side of the Atlantic, the American philosopher Charles Sanders Peirce was simultaneously and independently devising a "science of signs" which he called semiotics. Today the terms "semiotics" and "semiology" are often used interchangeably, though a few scholars have maintained that there are shades of difference between them. Peirce might have had a stronger influence on structuralism, were it not for the fact that the First World War fairly effectively broke down communication between European and American scholars at the very time when Saussure's thinking was making its primary impact on European linguists. Peirce was always reluctant to publish, and his pragmatic philosophy was as a rule coolly received by those European savants who were acquainted with it. Though Peirce died in 1914, the year

after Saussure's death, recognition of his importance was delayed until the publication of his major essays in 1923. The work of such men as Franz Boas, Edward Sapir and Leonard Bloomfield underlies what came in the United States to be called "structural linguistics," though it was not "structuralist" in the same sense in which that word was used by Troubetzkoy and Jakobson, or by Louis Hjelmslev of the "glossematic" school in Copenhagen. Quite apart from any other consideration, American structural linguists, unlike European structuralists, had not been under the influence of Russian formalism.

No scholar has so far succeeded in providing a definition of structuralism which is universally acceptable. It is not a philosophy, though it has often been called an epistemological point of view. It is based on the principle that every concept in a given system is determined by all other concepts of that system and has no significance by itself alone. Historically, structuralism is the application of principles derived from Saussurian linguistics to other areas of academic discourse. The forms of application have developed into complex methodologies, all of which have their advantages and disadvantages and reflect their formulator's peculiar ways of viewing the structuralist enterprise.

There is considerable disagreement on whether or not structuralism is a science.[1] Nowadays it is often categorized, at least when applied to language, as a derivative of what used to be called semiotic, a term which was originally used in medical science in connection with the theory of symptoms. Locke understood by the Greek word Σημειωτική a science of signs and significations. Saussure in his *Cours de Linguistique Générale* indicated on numerous occasions that he regarded linguistics as a science. Subsequently A.J. Greimas placed heavy emphasis on the use of scientific method in structuralist procedures, though his book *Sémantique Structurale* did not propose a logically formalized system of semantics. The Russian Formalists, especially Viktor Shklovsky, Boris Eichenbaum, Roman Jakobson in his Russian period, Juri Tynyanov and Boris Tomashevsky, gave structuralism a distinctly "literary" character, and in the process used the term

humanistically rather than in a strictly scientific fashion. Some modern structuralist have been forthright in maintaining that structural analysis is *not* a science. Roland Barthes, for example, in the introductory remarks to his analysis of Genesis 32, vv. 22-32 (Jacob's struggle with the angel) maintained that structural analysis "is certainly not a science, nor even a discipline."[2] The structuralist enterprise, considered as a whole, has thus a manifestly hybrid nature. Whether structuralism is regarded as an art or a science, at its heart is the idea of system: a complete, self-regulating entity that adapts to new conditions by transforming its features, while retaining its essential methodological character.

The problem of disentangling the scientific and artistic aspects of structuralism may perhaps be clarified by a musical analogy. A conductor, in interpreting a symphony in a certain way, is practising an art; yet he has also to understand and adapt to the acoustics of the concert hall in which he is conducting. Acoustics is not an art, but a branch of applied physics. The work of a conductor, therefore, involves factors which are both artistic and scientific. Likewise the structuralist should be simultaneously both artist and scientist. To continue the musical analogy, one may say that the structuralist reads the Bible in a manner roughly comparable to reading a musical score. In the case of a score, one reads the melody horizontally from left to right and the harmony vertically from top to bottom of the stave. Similarly (for the structuralist) the horizontal or diachronic reading of a biblical text manifests its "story," while the vertical or synchronic reading reveals its deep structure. In order to unconver the deep structure, the text must be formalized. Hence the importance of formalization in structuralist methodology, a scientific procedure that has no precise counterpart in other branches of biblical scholarship, but was much emphasized by logical positivists, who developed the concept of formalization with very considerable rigor and precision. In Lévi-Strauss's terminology, the purpose of formalization is to clarify "*paquets de relations*" or "bundles of relationships."

There are several ways of formalizing a text, all ultimately based on the general premiss that the structuralist is interested (in

Barthes' words) "not in the truth of the text but in its plurality." One method of procedure available to the structuralist is that of fitting the text to a grid composed of intersecting horizontal and vertical axes. In such a grid, each horizontal axis (or syntagm) presents the words of a text in their natural order, while each vertical axis (or paradigm) is composed of elements from other texts which have some kind of correlation to or something in common with the initial text. Thus there can be built up from these texts a hypothetical model for purposes of comparison, once the relationships among them have been established, and the common elements among them have emerged.

Another procedure is to decompose the content of the initial text into the various codes or figures inherent in it. ("Codes" is the term used by Barthes; "figures" is the term used by Gérard Genette.) The action of these codes or figures then becomes the main subject of analysis. What Barthes does with them is called (in Robert Scholes's terminology) high structuralism; what Genette does is called low structuralism.[3] Both procedures involve the investigation and analysis of different kinds of connotations. The terms "syntagm" and "paradigm" are also used in connection with the development of Saussure's methodology by his followers. His prototypal model was extended, with some modification, via two related "strategies": the *paradigmatic*, which led to Jakobson's structural phonology, and the *syntagmatic*, which led to Chomsky's generative syntax and to Philip Pettit's differential semantics. Syntagmatic strategy is linear in concept, and is generally visualized as a horizontal axis along which the individual words of a sentence are spread out. Hence in syntagmatic strategy, the meaning of a single word is determined by its position in a sentence. Syntagmatic strategy is especially appropriate to those languages with relatively few case endings. Paradigmatic strategy is vertical in concept. In this strategy the meaning of a single word is determined by its relation to those words which could have been used in its place and are, in a sense, invisibly present in a paradigmatic or vertical relationship to it. These other words will be generally synonyms. (The word "synonyms" is used loosely: there is no

such thing, strictly speaking, as an exact synonym because no two words have exactly the same connotation, though they may have the same denotation.)

Of the three basically Saussurean systems developed by Roman Jakobson, Noam Chomsky, and Philip Pettit, the latter's differential semantics has the advantage of not demanding a syntax which assigns a deep structure to every sentence; it does require a grasp of the surface structure, but it does not necessitate the use of the sentence or the categorical proposition as the basic semantic unit. The pericope or the textual lexie may in some circumstances be a much more convenient and appropriate type of division, and can be used in Pettit's system as the basic unit.[4]

Jakobson's structural phonology, Chomsky's generative syntax, and Pettit's differential semantics, considered as three aspects of the Saussurean linguistic model, may be used as a homeomorph or a paramorph, according to whether or not the subject of the model is also its source. If used homeomorphically, the Saussurean linguistic model results in stylistic analysis. If used paramorphically, the model can be, and often is, applied to non-literary arts. The idea of a methodology derived from linguistic structure being applied outside the literary field may seem strange to some literary critics. But anyone conversant with the anthropology of Claude Lévi-Strauss, the psychiatric theories of Jacques Lacan on the structure of the unconscious, or Marc Barbut's concepts of structure in mathematics is well aware that "structure" has a general applicability wherever there are methodologically analyzable entities.

It is important in this connection to remember that the word "structure" as used in structuralist theory differs from its meaning in rhetorical criticism, though there is some degree of overlap. "Structure" in rhetorical criticism generally means "pattern" or "arrangement." The word may have a syntactical connotation, when it refers to the structure of a sentence, or it may have an organizational innuendo, when it refers to a larger literary unit, such as a biblical book. In this second case the structure of the unit may appropriately be revealed by an outline of the text,

which may in some cases be intended to reproduce the original plan of an author.

The word "structure" as used by structuralists, on the other hand, does not refer primarily to the internal organization or arrangement of a text. Dan Via has provided one of the best definitions of "structure" in the structuralist sense: "Structure, properly speaking, is the hidden or underlying configuration that can offer some explanation for the more or less visible or obvious pattern in the text. Thus the goal of structuralist analysis or criticism is not to lead the work back to its origins or to reproduce the original plan of the author, but to produce a new knowledge. Structure is applied from outside and is not derived from the book; the book belongs to the structure without containing it. The work's meaning is not found inside it but beside it, at its limits, at the point where the text is joined to its structure."[5] In my opinion this definition is more explicit than the earlier and much quoted definition of "structure" provided by Emile Benveniste in his *Problems in General Linguistics*: "'Structure' is a whole formed of mutually dependent elements, such that each depends on the others and can only be what it is by its relationship to them."

Structuralism, then, derives from linguistics a framework of concepts which it seeks to extend from language to other areas of knowledge; e.g., literature, phonology, and anthropology. This framework of concepts constitutes a linguistic model, and the arguments for its extension to other areas of scholarship are conceptual or philosophical in nature. They collectively support the general proposition that where there is meaning there is structure; thus if language were not constructed, and if the use of language were not bound by rules, speakers could not give a common meaning to words and sentences.

Theory of meaning is a branch of philosophy rather than of literary criticism. Hence the relationship between a signifier and a signified is a semantical one, even though it is necessarily arbitrary and subjective. It corresponds to comparable relationships in the philosophy of logical positivism and especially of *der Wiener Kreis*: indeed, what Saussure called a *signifier* and Hjelmslev

called an *expression*, seems to me to correspond fairly closely to what Rudolf Carnap called a *designator*; and what Saussure called a *signified* and Hjelmslev called a *content*, corresponds to Carnap's *designatum.*

The identification of a system of "signs" is also common to logical positivism, Saussurean linguistics, and structuralism. In the history of logical positivism, the distinction between logical and descriptive signs led to two different identification procedures represented by Carnap and Tarski. Carnap emphasized in his *Formalization of Logic* and elsewhere the distinction between semantics and syntax, i.e., between semantical systems as interpreted language systems and purely formal, uninterpreted calculi, while for Tarski there was no such distinction. Saussure did not make this distinction either: his first priority was to counter the nominalist view that words have meaning through standing as names of things. His argument led him eventually to the conclusion that structure is essentially "differential." Chomsky later argued to the effect that structure is essentially "generative." These positions, incidentally, are not mutually exclusive, and can be maintained simultaneously. On the basis of his distinctions between synchrony and diachrony and between *langue* and *parole,* Saussure's contention seems to me to be valid. Chomsky was arguing equally validly, but in a different direction, when he described generative grammar as a system of rules that can generate an indefinitely large number of structures. Generative structure, then, plays the role, *mutatis mutandis* in Chomsky's thinking that differential structure plays in Saussure's. Both types of structuralism, differential and generative, are applicable to the text of sacred scripture.

The use of structuralist methods in biblical studies is, in a sense, a reaction against the kind of mentality engendered by *Formgeschichte* and *Redaktionsgeschichte*. Roland Frye, T.R. Henn, and other scholars in the humanities have chosen to concentrate on the final literary work itself, the *textus completus,* its rhetorical features, and its different kinds of structures. The final text of the Bible, conflated though it is in some portions, is a completed,

canonized whole which is more than the sum of its component parts. Unlike the form critic and the redaction critic, the rhetorical critic and the structuralist are both concerned primarily with the finished textual product rather than the separate ingredients which went into its making. Or, from another point of view, the structuralist is interested in analyzing the *art* in the biblical text, rather than investigating the documents that lie behind it or the manner in which the editorial conflation took place.

However, the results of structuralist research may well seem odd to other biblical scholars, partly because they are couched in terminology different from their own, and partly because they seem (to at least some biblical exegetes), somewhat exiguous in relation to the amount of theory that went into producing them. It is sometimes suggested that structuralists are more interested in their theories than in whatever conclusions may follow from their application. Critical hypotheses involving grids, strings, vectors, phase-spaces, and different kinds of "fluidities" may cause a biblical scholar to feel a virtual foreigner in the land of the structuralists. However, the constant use of a linguistic model in structuralist procedure is not (as one critic has claimed) "a bizarre piece of French nonsense lacking all sense of historical dimension." Structuralists have arrived at some valuable and (I think) reasonable conclusion. Most structuralists today would agree that the Bible contains a complex network of structures; for example, linguistic structures in general, with a hierarchy of structures of systems of macro-signs, and semiotic structures of content, including a narrative system and a mythical system. These structures can be analyzed in a kind of mathematical reduction of the text, which should result in a clarification of their constants and variables.

Analytic procedures used by structuralists working on the biblical text differ considerably, but there are four general, fundamental principles which underlie at least the most significant structuralist methodologies:

1. The structuralist is not *primarily* concerned with the meaning of a text (in the usual sense of the word "meaning") or with

its previous history, or with what its author or authors intended it to mean. Instead, he sees the text as a manifestation of
various kinds of structures (semantic, linguistic, narrative,
mythical, etc.), and analyzes it in terms of these structures.
He assumes that the "value of a language" (to use Saussure's
terminology) is to be found only in the structures.

2. The structures of a particular text are the semantic potentialities of this text.
3. The structuralist's approach generally should be synchronic
   and paradigmatic rather than diachronic and syntagmatic.
4. Structuralist methodologies are intended to *complement*
   other procedures for analyzing the biblical text and not to
   supplant them.

While these principles are held in common among most structuralists, differences of approach sometimes mean differences in
understanding the basis of literary structure. According to Barthes
for example, the basis of the structure must be sought in the
character of the process of writing itself; according to Lévi-
Strauss and Greimas, it must be sought in the structure of the
thought process; according to Güttgemanns, who is concerned
with literary structure primarily in the context of New Testament
theology, it should be sought in the theory of generative poetic.

Lévi-Strauss's methodology is based on structural phonological
theory. According to him, the semantic content of myths can be
reduced to pairs of binary oppositions which reflect the fundamental logical structure of human thought processes. Hence the
underlying meaning of myth should be seen as the struggle of a
culture to find ways to mediate logical contradictions inherent
in its literary traditions as well as in its cultural psyche. Greimas,
using the narrative functionalism of Vladimir Propp, developed
phonological binarism into a semantic theory, and related this
theory to narrative syntax. Hence he demonstrated that the
diachronic structure of a narrative is also generated by logical
binary oppositions at the semantic level. The actants of a narrative,
he proposed, are mythical representations of logical operations,
and can be reduced to a standard actantial model. In his favour it

must be admitted that relations in many biblical narratives correspond well to this model.

Barthes was strongly influenced by Marx and Freud, a fact that
is clear from *Le Degré Zéro de l'Écriture,* in its English version
Writing Degree Zero, which appeared in 1953. He sees the *écriture
classique* of seventeenth-century France as being not a conscious
style, but a "way" of writing which was for its practitioners the
only right way. Later bourgeois *écriture* was likewise the only
right way of composition for bourgeois authors. Subsequent
attempts to write in a styleless manner by such authors as Camus
and Hemingway have merely proved that stylelessness may itself
become a style. Such considerations as these led Barthes to the
conclusion that writing is all style: there is not such entity as
writing without some kind of style. He defines writing as a free
act accomplished in relation to fixed, Oedipally determined
linguistic codes and socially determined literary codes. However,
when writing does not surrender to closed, socially sanctioned or
Oedipally determined meaning, its language acquires an emancipat-
ing power, both socially and personally. Barthes thus seeks to
understand the structure of a narrative in terms of its difference
from rather than in its conformity to a fixed model. Hence the
importance in Barthes' methodology of the psychoanalytic "paradigm of the difference."

Barthes also amplified the Saussurian concept of signs. Saussure
had argued that linguistics is only a part of the semiological
enterprise:

Semiology should show what constitutes signs, what laws govern them. Since
the science does not yet exist, no one can say what it would be; but it has a
right to existence, a place staked out in advance. Linguistics is only a part of
the general science of semiology. . . .[6]

In his *Elements of Semiology* Barthes proposed to treat all cultural
complexes as systems of signs, thereby subsuming that human
culture in general is interpretable by means of a vast structure of
such sign systems. This concept of universal semantization rests on

the premise that all entities within human culture can be invested with some degree of meaning of signification.

The approaches of Lévi-Strauss and Greimas on the one hand, and that of Barthes on the other present the Biblical scholar with the possibility of dealing systematically with the semantic level of the biblical narrative, while at the same time understanding the structure of the narrative as the outgrowth of a paradigmatic "generative" model. The choice between these two approaches is a choice between a binary semantic paradigm which excludes the historical subject, and one which portrays the generative structure of the historical subject.

The methodology of Güttgemanns is in many respects radically different from that of Barthes and Greimas, while plainly deriving some of its inspiration from Saussure and Lévi-Strauss. Yet his notion of Gattung is not essentially different from Barthes' *signified* or Todorov's *genre*: he seems to see *Gattungen* as inherent structures of the human mind. There is an indeterminate number of *Gattungen*, but it is theoretically possible that all of them may be conceptually articulated within the context of generative poetic by structural analysis. On the basis of such analysis, Güttgemanns has developed a novel and rather idiosyncratic New Testament theology, which he regards as a science of texts about God.

The methodologies of Lévi-Strauss, Barthes, Greimas, and Güttgemanns are today the best established structuralist procedures for analyzing the biblical text. They will therefore be discussed in greater detail in the chapters which follow.

Notes

1.   A valuable discussion of the matter from a historical point of view is provided by Ernest Gellner in his article "What is Structuralism?" in *The Times Literary Supple-*

ment, July 31, 1981, pp. 881 ff. For an older but solid essay on the same matter see Peter Caws, "What is Structuralism?" in *Partisan Review*, Vol. 35, 1968, pp. 75-91.

2. Alfred M. Johnson, trans., *Structural Analysis and Biblical Exegesis* (Pittsburgh: Pickwick Press, 1974), p. 21. As will be explained in Chapter III, note 2, I have used the "Protestant" verse numbering in discussing Barthes' treatment of this pericope from Genesis 32, which deals with the story of Jacob at Penuel.

3. Other higher structuralist procedures include, according to Scholes, the methodologies of Michel Foucault and Jacques Lacan. See Robert Scholes, *Structuralism in Literature* (New Haven: Yale University Press, 1974), p. 157.

4. See Philip Pettit, *The Concept of Structuralism: A Critical Analysis* (Berkeley: University of California Press, 1975), especially Ch. IV, "The Value of the Model," pp. 100-117. Pettit's comment, "What Structuralism derives from the linguistic model is primarily a metaphysic" (p. 113) deserves considering in contradistinction to those definitions of structuralism (e.g., by Greimas and Derrida) limiting it solely to a scientific context and thereby denying it any metaphysical content.

5. Dan Via, *Kerygma and Comedy in the New Testament: A Structuralist Approach to Hermeneutic* (Philadelphia: Fortress Press, 1975), p. 7. For my review of this book see *Theological Studies*, Vol. 36 (September 1975), pp. 558 f.

6. Ferdinand de Saussure, *Course in General Linguistics* translated by Wade Baskin (New York: McGraw-Hill, 1966), p. 16. The original is best read in Saussure's *Course de Linguistique Générale*, edited by Rudolf Engler (Wiesbaden: Otto Harrassowitz, 1967). Hugh Bredin has argued that Saussure's theory of linguistic signs is "an ontology." See Hugh Bredin, "Sign and Value in Saussure," *Philosophy*, Vol. 59 (1984), pp. 67-77.

The Methodology of Claude Lévi-Strauss

The earliest methodology to be used for structuralist analysis of the biblical text originated with Lévi-Strauss's collection of papers published in 1958 under the title *Anthropologie Structurale*, especially the celebrated eleventh chapter, "La Structure des Mythes."[1] Lévi-Strauss did not apply his own methods directly to Hebrew mythology, but he did provide the foundations for later scholars who used it to analyze initially the mythical material in Genesis, and subsequently other portions of the sacred text.

Lévi-Strauss first notes the similarity between myths collected in widely differing regions, despite the fact that the conventions of everyday reality are not consistently followed in myth. This fact, he comments, may be compared to a similar phenomenon in language: different languages use much the same restricted collection of phonemes, but at the same time differ greatly among. themselves. Just as meaning arises in language from the combination of arbitrary phonemes, so meaning in myth should arise not from the intrinsic meaning of the actions, but from their combination. However, language and myth differ from each other in several ways, one of which becomes clear in relation to Lévi-Strauss's celebrated definition of myth as "the part of language where the formula *traduttore, traditore* reaches its lowest truth value."[2] By that statement he meant that the essential value of myth is preserved even through the worst translation; poetry, on the other hand, cannot be translated (he claimed) except at the cost of serious distortion. The substance of myth does not lie in its style or syntax, but in the *story* which it tells. This principle (he further claimed) is emphatically not true of poetry.

Myth contains both *langue* and *parole*, two terms which were first distinguished by Saussure, and which are roughly comparable to Hjelmslev's *schema* and *usage*, Chomsky's more recent expressions *competence* and *performance*, or to *code* and *message* of

the information theorists. *Langue,* according to Saussure, is the socially ordered aspect of speech, or the sum of word-images stored in the minds of all individuals who speak the same language. It comprises numerous systems of rules, e.g., phonological, grammatical and syntactical, which can be used in restrictive, combinative and other fashions. *Parole,* on the other hand, is speaking itself, or the individual's actualization of the collective potential of the *langue. Langue* and *parole* are interdependent; the former is both the instrument and the product of the latter. In myth, *langue* is bound to reversible time, and its nature is synchronic; *parole* in myth belongs to non-reversible time, and its nature is diachronic. Myth as a whole, therefore, unites synchrony and diachrony in that it is told in past time, and yet it has a real effect on the present. Furthermore myth is composed of actions with a similarity to one another. Between these actions are relations. The minimum significant units, analogous to words, are "bundles of such relations." The "bundles" amount to paradigms, of which the individual relations are connected to one another by the principle of similarity. "Relations pertaining to the same bundle may appear diachronically at remote intervals," wrote Lévi-Strauss, "but when we have succeeded in grouping them together we have reorganized our myth according to a time referent of a new nature, . . . namely a two dimensional time referent which is simultaneously diachronic and syncronic, and which accordingly integrates the characteristics of *langue* on the one hand, and those of *parole* on the other."[3]

One of Lévi-Strauss's working assumptions, then, was that myth is made up of constituent units, and that these units, which are to be found on the sentence level, presuppose the constituent units present in language when it is analyzed on lower levels; e.g., phonemes, morphemes, and sememes. Sentences differ from these lower level units, being more complex. Lévi-Strauss refers to sentences in myth as *gross constituent units* or *mythemes.* A *mytheme* can be symbolized as follows:

$$F_x (a)$$

This formula should be read: Every *mytheme* expresses the concept that a certain function [*prédicat*] "x" is at a given time linked to a given subject "a." In actual practice, of course, Lévi-Strauss's formula can be appropriately applied only to relatively simple narratives: in more complex narratives the mythemes become in effect macro-mythemes which are parts of an entire system of macro-mythemes related to other kinds of systems at different structural levels.

It is clear that Lévi-Strauss was not so much concerned with the "expression" of mythological texts as with their "contents." His procedure in analyzing a myth was to break down its story into the shortest possible sentences, and to write each sentence on an index card bearing a number corresponding to the unfolding of the story. Almost every card, he claimed, showed that a certain function was at a given time linked to a given subject, or in other words, each gross constituent unit consisted of a relation. The true constituent units of a myth, he concluded, are bundles of such relations, for only as bundles can these relations be combined to produce a meaning.

It is appropriate at this point to make three observations on Lévi-Strauss's methodology which will be relevant to structuralist exegesis of scripture in general. First, the use of this method necessitates the maintenance of a dialectical tension between the diachronic and synchronic approaches to the biblical text. The structuralist normally uses a methodologically synchronic approach, but that fact does not mean that he is limited to a specific time span: for this reason the term *achronic* is sometimes used instead of *synchronic*. He may enrich his analysis of a particular structure by comparing it to other structures which do not belong to the same time span. In doing so he has no temporal concern, since in an absolute sense the time sequence has no relevance. Indeed, time can be viewed as reversible at the structural level. In a structuralist analysis of a particular portion of the Bible, intertextual correlations may well be used for comparative purposes: whether the texts used for comparison were written before or after the text under analysis is a consideration of no importance.

This ahistorical and adiachronic type of exegesis is necessarily characterized by a specific concept of time as being non-linear.

Secondly, Lévi-Strauss throughout his work maintains that a myth is made up of all its variants. He perceives myth as involving a system of mythological texts, i.e., a system of mythical signs (or macro-signs) in which each mythological text is to be viewed as a sign. The mythical structure is the structure of this system of mythical signs. After the presence of the mythical structure is recognized, it must still be identified. This identification is best made by studying myths in the same "group" together: a "group" consists of all the mythological texts of a given culture.

Thirdly, the mythological texts are not the *only* mythical signs. A myth mediates fundamental, metaphysical oppositions through a theoretically infinite number of secondary oppositions which are amenable to a mediation. Collectively, as Lévi-Strauss demonstrated in his *Mythologiques,* these secondary oppositions embrace most aspects of the culture of any given society. Hence a myth derives from a culture as a whole: it is not simply the set of the culture's mythological texts. Furthermore, the mythical structure is at work in texts which are not mythological, e.g., the Pauline letters. This consideration will be developed later in this chapter.

The first scholar to attempt a structuralist type of analysis of a biblical myth was the anthropologist Sir Edmund Leach, who published his initial results in 1961. He was avowedly influenced by the methods of Lévi-Strauss. As his subject he chose the creation myth in the early chapters of Genesis, and provided a structural analysis of the creation stories in his essay entitled "Lévi-Strauss in the Garden of Eden."[4] Leach relates his analysis to communications theory, singling out the elements of *redundancy* and *binary opposition*. Redundancy arises from the fact that "all important stories recur in several versions." Binarism, which is "intrinsic to the process of human thought" is the discrimination of opposing categories which are mutually exclusive. The three most relevant binary oppositions or antinomies are life versus death, male versus female, and human versus divine.

According to Leach, religion everywhere is preoccupied with

the antinomy of life versus death:

Religion seeks to deny the binary link between the two words; it does this by creating the mystical idea of 'another world,' a land of the dead where life is perpetual. . . . The central 'problem' of religion is then to re-establish some kind of bridge between man [in this world] and God [in the other]. This pattern is built into the structure of every mythical system; the myth first discriminates between gods and men and then becomes preoccupied with the relations and intermediaries which link men and gods together.[5]

Leach further maintains that in every mythical system there is "a persistent sequence of binary discriminations" between such opposites as human/superhuman, mortal/immortal, good/bad, male/female, legitimate/illegitimate, and so on. These paired categories are bridged in almost every myth by some form of "mediation," in the form of abnormal or anomalous entities, e.g., incarnate gods, virgin mothers, or semi-divine monsters. They inhabit a middle ground which is abnormal, non-natural, and holy. This middle ground is typically the focus of all taboo and ritual observance. Leach supports these contentions with examples of primitive myths taken directly from the works of Lévi-Strauss.

Together with the binary opposition which Leach finds inherent in these myths, he also perceives redundancy. The value of redundancy to the structural anthropologist is that it corrects errors introduced through "noise", i.e., those elements of a message which are accidental to meaning. Meaningful relations are distinguished from noise by their presence in a pattern observable through all the variants of the narrative.

Leach provides an elaborate diagram intended to summarize the binary distinctions and mediations of the creation myth, which in accordance with the principle of redundancy appears in three permutations: what biblical scholars call the J and P creation stories and the story of Cain and Abel. The P creation story, he maintains, is divisible into two three-day periods, the first characterized by the creation of the static or "dead" world, the second by the creation of the moving, sexual, "live" world. Just as the static triad of grass, cereals, and fruit trees is created on the third day,

the triad of domestic and wild animals and creeping things appears on the sixth, "but only the grass is allocated to the animals. Everything else, including the meat of the animals, is for man's use." Finally, man and woman are created simultaneously and commanded to be fruitful and multiply, "but the problems of life versus death and incest versus procreation are not faced at all."

The J creation story exhibits, according to Leach, a number of structural similarities to the P account. For example, the creation of Eve (in J) is comparable to that of the creeping things (in P) because both create oppositions, the creeping things to the other animals and Eve to the man. The serpent, a creeping thing, is the mediator between man and woman. When Adam and Eve eat the forbidden fruit, death and (according to Leach) the capacity for the procreation of life enter the world together. The story of Cain and Abel repeats the earlier oppositions. Abel, the herdsman, represents the living world; Cain, the tiller of the ground, represents the static. Cain's fratricide is a reprise of Adam's incest: as Adam had to eliminate a sister in order to acquire a wife, so Cain must eliminate a brother.

Leach's application of Lévi-Strauss's methodology is open to a number of criticisms. Among them are the following:

1. Leach uses as his single authoritative text the translation in the King James Version (KJV) of 1611. He does not utilize the original Hebrew text at any point in his argument. This procedure leads to a few misinterpretations, one of which is the implication based on the KJV translation of Genesis 1:29 that Adam and Eve were meat-eaters. The ambiguous phrase "for meat" in the KJV translates the Hebrew l^e *oklah* which can only mean "for food" in modern English. The implication of Genesis 1:29, 30 in the original Hebrew is that mankind was restricted to a vegetarian diet; a meat diet was permitted only in the Noachic period, as is clear in Genesis 9:1-3. Such solecisms as these serve to corroborate the general principle that an examination of Hebrew myth cannot rest on any particular translation.

2.   When Lévi-Strauss used the term *myth* he did not intend it to include written material.[6] Still less did he intend it to include material which contains several layers of writing which were subsequently edited. Once a myth is written down, it ceases to be a product of the unconscious generative force in the society that produced it, and becomes instead the report of that force acting upon given materials at one particular moment. It is debatable, therefore, to what extent the edited P and J materials in the early chapters of Genesis collectively constitute a valid example of "myth" in Lévi-Strauss's sense of the term. The assumption behind a Lévi-Straussian analysis of a myth is that the audience of the myth is aware, if only "unconsciously," of the permutations and transformations of the myth; once a myth assumes a written form it becomes crystalized, a product of its culture which no longer undergoes such permutations and transformations. Leach employed Lévi-Strauss's basic approach in the same debatable manner as a number of other structuralists subsequently did: he used it on "literate" texts, although it was intended by Lévi-Strauss himself to be used on "oral" texts. There is today no general agreement on the psychodynamic differences between orality and literacy, but they surely exist and should ideally be taken into consideration in structural analysis.

3.   The writers of the early chapters of Genesis had aims very different from those of most transmitters of mythic materials. Their aim was to correct existing Babylonian and Canaanite polytheistic teachings rather than to create a new mythology. This fact is especially clear in the case of the P creation story which, though it rests on a number of mythical assumptions (e.g., direct creation of living beings by God), is to a degree anti-mythological. The Priestly writer gives every impression of composing a piece of explicit monotheistic polemic against the Babylonian polytheistic myth of creation contained in *Enuma Elish*. If he did his work in Babylon during the Babylonian captivity, as is highly probable, he would have had a strong motive for adopting a defensive attitude against his

Babylonian captors and their mythology. Regarded in this light, the account of creation in Genesis might be described, in terms of genre, as an example of anti-myth rather than myth.

4. Leach sees the story of Adam, Eve, Cain, and Abel as being a variation of the same theme that occurs in the Oedipus myth: the parallels between the two myths, he remarks, are "too close to be accidental." In my opinion the parallels could well be fortuitous: there is no evidence that either J or P was acquainted with Greek mythology. However, Leach presents a number of literary parallels in some detail. He comments that Oedipus, like Adam and Cain, is "initially earthbound and immobile," but in the end he is, like Cain, an exiled wandered protected by the gods. The serpent of Genesis has as its counterpart the sphinx of the Oedipus myth. Eve listens to the serpent's words and betrays Adam into what Leach calls "incest": likewise Oedipus solves the riddle of the sphinx prior to *his* being led into incest. This attempt to balance Oedipus's patricide against Cain's fratricide seems to me to be forced: there is no provable significance in the assertion that Adam, Cain, and Oedipus were all "initially earthbound and immobile," the sphinx serves an entirely different purpose from the serpent of Genesis, and there is nothing in the J text to imply that Adam and Eve were expelled from Eden on account of the sin of incest. Furthermore, Leach's attempt to interpret Genesis 4:7 as evidence of homosexual incest between Cain and Abel is highly dubious. It rests entirely on the KJV translation of the admittedly enigmatic Hebrew original. The KJV reads thus:

If man doest well, shalt thou not be accepted? And if thou doest not well, sin lieth at the door. And unto thee shall be his desire, and thou shalt rule over him.

The NEB translation is preferable, if one accepts the necessary vowel changes which it reflects in the masoretic text. It allows

no possibility of being interpreted as evidence of homosexual incest:

> If you do well, you are accepted, if not, sin is a demon crouching at the door. It shall be eager for you, and you will be mastered by it.

5. Some of the oppositions which Leach sees in J and P creation stories seem deliberately selected in order to buttress his thesis. It is true that one can validly posit an opposition between creeping things and other animals in P, but clearly it is not the same *kind* of opposition as that which exists between man and woman in J. A number of his other oppositions seem questionable for essentially the same reason: they involve different kinds, and therefore do not incorporate logically valid opposites.

6. Leach's treatment of incest in the Garden of Eden is questionable, and seems to presuppose a system of post-Edenic morality in Eden itself. Since the pericope under discussion nowhere mentions incest, the introduction of the subject here seems to be anthropologically irrelevant. The authors of the biblical account no doubt held moral beliefs on the subject of incest, but refrained from reading them backwards into the Edenic period. The claim that Cain's fratricide was a reprise of Adam's incest seems to suggest that the murder of Abel was motivated solely by the incestuousness of the father of both killer and victim. This type of explanation is not exegesis of the biblical text, but eisegesis.

It is reasonable to doubt, therefore, whether Leach's application of Lévi-Strauss's structuralist principles to the early chapters of Genesis is successful. It led Lévi-Strauss himself to express misgivings about the suitability of applying structuralist methodology to the text of the Hebrew Bible.[7] "The Old Testament," he maintained, "which certainly does make use of mythical materials, takes them up with a view to a different end from their original one." His contention, which was shared by Paul Ricoeur, is that the *purpose* of the biblical writers was different from that of the

originators of the mythical materials which they used. These materials were subject to an "intellectual operation," and were deliberately inserted into a confessional framework. One may, I believe, deduce from this objection of Lévi-Strauss and Ricoeur that the early chapters of Genesis are, in their view, not primarily mythological. Once this fact is granted, it is reasonable to question the validity of subjecting them to an analysis the presuppositions of which are at best only partially appropriate to them.

The attempt of Leach to apply Lévi-Strauss's methodology to the early chapters of Genesis makes patently manifest one of the principal disadvantages of structuralist exegesis: it must start on the hypothetical premiss that the biblical text is a synchronous whole. This fact creates problems for the structuralist dealing with historically multi-layered or conflated portions of the biblical text. For this reason it has been argued, paradoxically, that Lévi-Strauss's methods, properly adapted and augmented, may sometimes work better on non-mythical portions of the sacred text. Of those scholars who have produced structuralist analyses of such biblical segments using the methodology of Lévi-Strauss, undoubtedly one of the foremost is Daniel Patte. His analyses of Galatians I:1-10, and the parable of the Good Samaritan will be considered in some detail.[8]

In his exegesis of Galatians I:1-10, Patte rightly maintains that mythical structures can be discerned in non-mythological texts. The Pauline epistles are collections of theological arguments. Such arguments are, in Patte's term, "religious meaning effects," and are produced by the unconscious interaction of deep structures and by a specific actualization of mythical structure.[9] A theological argument is undoubtedly more concise than a mythological text, which is generally characterized by redundancies. St. Paul often expresses the potential subject matter of one or more mythological stories in a few phrases or single terms incorporated into a piece of logical polemic. These phrases and terms represent "bundles of mythemes" or "broad mythemes."

In order to discover the broad mythemes in the Epistle to the Galatians two initial steps are necessary.

1. The expansion of St. Paul's text: every pertinent phrase or term should be expressed as a broad mytheme in the form of a short sentence.
2. A second expansion to express the mythemes themselves. (Patte does not perform this second expansion.)

It should be noted that the exegete does not in this case proceed to the two reductions required for the analysis of a mythological text; i.e., the syntagmatic reduction of each part of the story into a mytheme and the paradigmatic reduction of each bundle of mythemes into one broad mytheme.

Another special feature of a theological argument is that in it the fundamental opposition is assumed to have been mediated. In the case of myth, convictions are in the process of being established; in a theological argument they are assumed to have been established. As a result, a theological argument exhibits the same mythical structure as the corresponding myth, but manifests the opposite "orientation." In a myth, a first opposition is mediated by another, more secondary, opposition, and the position of mediator in the first opposition occupies the positive pole of the following opposition. (The positive pole of an opposition is that pole which is also the mediator of another opposition.) In a theological argument, by contrast, the orientation is from the fundamental opposition towards the secondary oppositions. The mediation of the fundamental opposition permits the mediation of the secondary oppositions. It will be clear that the series of oppositions in each case remains the same, even though the mediations are seen in two opposite ways. In the theological argument the mediating terms result from the constraints of a structure of the enunciation: they are the positive poles of fundamental oppositions. In the mythical structure the mediating terms are the positive poles of the more secondary oppositions.

Galatians presents the conflict between two principal mythical structures: Paul's gospel and the anti-gospel of his opponents. Other mythical structures are also represented in the text; e.g., the Pharisaic mythical structure and a Hellenistic mythical structure. Lévi-Strauss's model, with a little adaptation, can be used

to incorporate all four structures. It is appropriate to symbolize them thus:

S^1 :   The mythical structure "Paul's gospel."

S^2 :   The Pharisaic mythical structure.

S^3 :   The Hellenistic mythical structure.

S^4 :   The "anti-gospel" mythical structure.

If S^2 and S^3 are parts of S^1 they must belong to its negative side. If they were to belong to its positive side, the implication would be that Paul's gospel was only a form of Pharisaic Judaism, or some kind of Hellenistic myth, or a combination of the two. The negative side of the structure is joined to the positive by the mediations. S^4, of course, is not joined to S^1 in this way. If the symbol $\equiv$ is used to indicate correlation, it follows that

$$S^4 \equiv S^3 \equiv S^2$$

Patte provides two detailed readings of the text of Galatians I:1-10, one syntagmatic and the other paradigmatic. His task is made difficult by the fact that St. Paul unsystematically mixes the different terminologies of the S^1, S^2, S^3, and S^4. If St. Paul had been a good structuralist, he would have spoken of the "anti-gospel" in terms of the Pharisaic and Hellenistic mythical structures, of Pharisaic Judaism in terms of the "anti-gospel" and Hellenistic mythical structures, and of the Galatians' former religion in terms of the "anti-gospel" and Pharisaic mythical structures. However, he does not maintain any such distinctions consistently. Patte's rather negative conclusion is that one may not validly make judgments on the specific doctrines of St. Paul's opponents solely from the fact that he uses a mixture of terminologies when writing about the "other gospel." The nature of this "other gospel" has to be investigated by other means.

An unsympathetic critic of structuralism might well make three responses to this conclusion:

1. It is largely common sense. No competent biblical exegete has ever argued that the nature of the "other gospel" could be ascertained simply from the fact that St. Paul in these ten verses uses a mixture of terminologies.

2. The complexity of the methodology and the length of the readings are hardly justified by so limited a conclusion.
3. It looks as if St. Paul's writings are here being forced into a structuralist strait jacket, and then criticized because they do not fit perfectly.

I believe that there would be an element of truth in these responses of the suppositional critic. Similar criticisms could be made of the majority of structuralist exegeses. Patte himself partially revised his procedures in *Structural Exegesis: From Theory to Practice* to provide for a greater degree of methodological precision. However, even under hypothetically ideal conditions, there are severe constraints on what can be achieved by structuralist methods. They should be used to complement other exegetical methods.

There are a few lacunae in Patte's syntagmatic and paradigmatic readings in *What is Structural Exegesis*? Once one accepts that fact that his exegesis is formulated within the general limits of the Lévi-Straussian method. Admittedly Patte is here concerned primarily with mythical structures but some references to the semantic structures within the text would have been welcome, together with comments on their connection to the relevant deep syntactical structures. These shortcomings are to some extent remedied in *Structural Exegesis: From Theory to Practice,* especially in Patte's discussions of the sociolectal semantic universe and the idiolectal semantic universe, but these systems are Greimasian in character rather than Lévi-Straussian. One also misses a complete analysis of the mythical structures of Pharisaism and Hellenism, especially in view of the fact that these systems function at the structural level as bundles of mythemes. The Pharisaic and Hellenistic mythical systems were, after all, the mythical systems to which most of the early Christians belonged before their conversion: hence arises their special significance in relation to the Pauline letters. In the course of the syntagmatic reading Patte identifies the broad mythemes in the text and manifests that a number of complete mythical systems have in this case to be viewed as broad mythemes of the gospel mythical structure. In the paradigmatic reading he demonstrates how the mythical

structure imposes its constraints upon the epistolary-theological argument at the textual surface. Incidentally, the same method when applied to other New Testament texts reveals quite different actualizations of the mythical structure, and thereby demonstrates the existence of a number of different gospel mythical structures.

By contrast to Galatians I:1-10, the parable of the Good Samaritan is an example of simple narrative. Unlike complex narrative, simple narrative actualizes only one opposition and eventually its mediation. The actualization of the mythical structure in a simple narrative involves only a limited number of broad mythemes or bundles of mythemes. For this reason the structural exegesis of parables is, in general, simpler than that of theological arguments.

Patte's brief analysis of the story of the Good Samaritan constitutes the basis of his conclusion that this story was a parable proposed as a paradigm for discovering the "signs of the Kingdom."[10] I emphasize my agreement with Patte that the story of the good Samaritan really is a *parable,* as against Bultmann and a number of other scholars, including the structuralist Dan Via, who have categorized it as an example story.[11] Via was actually arguing against an earlier paper of J.D. Crossan, who maintained that the Story of the Good Samaritan is a parable, and who reiterated his position in a subsequent rejoinder to Via's article. This sequence of three articles, something of a *cause célèbre* in the short history of structuralist scriptural polemic, is as follows:

1. J.D. Crossan, "Parable and Example in the Teaching of Jesus," *New Testament Studies*, Vol. 18 (1972), pp. 285-307.
2. Dan Via, "Parable and Example Story: A Literary-Structuralist Approach," *Linguistica Biblica*, Vol. 25/26 (1973), pp. 21-30; enlarged version in *Semeia*, Vol. 1 (1974), pp. 105-133.
3. J.D. Crossan, "Structuralist Analysis and the Parables of Jesus," *Linguistica Biblica*, Vol. 29/30 (1973), pp. 41-51; enlarged version in *Semeia*, Vol. 1 (1974), pp. 192-221.

The second issue of the journal *Semeia* (1974), edited by Crossan, was entirely devoted to the Good Samaritan and continued the discussion. A full appreciation of Via's argument requires a brief summary of Crossan's original position.

According to Crossan, a parable has two points, a literal one which stems from the surface level, and a metaphysical one which is based on a deeper level. An example story, by contrast, has only one point and one level. Crossan's general thesis is that what some authors have called "example stories" are actually parables whose literal level has been taken as a moral injunction, and whose deeper, metaphorical level has been missed or ignored. Applied to the Good Samaritan, Crossan's case is that the literal point is the shocking and unexpected juxtaposition of Samaritan (10:33) and good neighbour (10:36); the metaphorical point is that the Kingdom of God abruptly breaks into a person's consciousness, over-turning former established values. Crossan adds that one must have some idea of Jesus' teaching from his non-symbolic state-ments in order to distinguish correctly between the literal and metaphorical meanings of his parables.

According to Via, there is not enough semantic tension or distance between Crossan's literal and metaphorical levels for the story of the Good Samaritan to be regarded as a metaphor of the Kingdom of God. It is a metaphor in the sense that it gives a new meaning to the responsibilities of neighbourliness, but this is not Crossan's contention. Furthermore, Crossan fails to observe the autonomy of the story: he confounds story and *discourse* in a case where the story is a discrete enclave within the discourse. For Via, narrative exists at the two levels of story and discourse. At the story level, narrative is objective statement creating a world of events and persons who are real from the viewpoint of that created world. Story is characterized by the use of the third person and the aorist and pluperfect tenses. At the discourse level, narrative is subjective articulation, spoken by a narrator to a hearer. Discourse is characterized by the use of "I" and "you," adverbs like "today," the present and future tenses, and evaluative statements. The narrative may be simultaneously story and dis-course; on the other hand either story or discourse may be a discrete enclave within the other, as happens in the case of the Good Samaritan.

Within the story level, several sub-levels may be distinguished.

Via describes two of these, the plot and actantial sub-levels, thereby grafting some of the principles of Greimas onto a basically Lévi-Straussian methodology. He compares the plot of the Good Samaritan to those of eight narrative parables of Jesus: the Prodigal Son, the Unjust Steward, the Wedding Feast, Lazarus and the Rich Man, the Pharisee and the Publican, the Rich Fool, the Wedding Guest, and the Workers in the Vineyard. These eight parables vary with regard to plot movement and episode pattern, but their separate plots always constitute an organic unity. In the Good Samaritan the plot is *not* an organic unity. The denouement is not a real denouement, and while all of the narrative parables exhibit what in Todorov's terms may be called sequential causality, it does not appear at all in the Good Samaritan.

Another problem arises over the question of the unit-limits. In his first article Crossan maintained that Luke 10:25-28 and 10:30-36 were originally separate. 10:37 is also an addition, he claimed, and it is 37b which turns the narrative into an example story. The unit which Crossan interprets as a parable is therefore 10:30-36. Its genre-parable is derived from the juxtaposition of Samaritan (10:33) and good neighbour (10-36). Via's complaint is that Crossan's derivation is based not on the story itself, but on the relationship of the story to Jesus' question to the scribe: "What is written in the Law? What is your reading of it?" (10:26). Hence it may be argued (as Via does) that Crossan's unit 10:30-36 is not a legitimate one for analysis. Luke 10:25-37 is a discrete unit of Luke's *story*, though it contains some elements of *discourse,* such as the evaluative statement that the scribe desired to justify himself (10:29a). Within Luke's *story* unit is Jesus' *discourse* with the scribe (10:25b-37), and within the discourse, the unit 10:30-35 (omitting "Jesus replied" in 10:30) is a discrete enclave of *story.* The decisions concerning where one closes a unit for analysis and where one opens it are logically reciprocal, as Louis Marin has shown.[12] It follows that, since Crossan chose not to include the discourse in 10:25b-29, structural logic forbids his including the discourse in 10:36. Consequently, Crossan's parabolic unit is invalid.

Crossan's counter-criticism is not entirely satisfactory. He accepts Luke 10:30b-35 as a discrete enclave of *story*, but insists that it is a parable and not an example story because it is "a metaphor-story [sic] of the Kingdom's advent as a world shattering event, from the *story* alone."[13] Since so much of Crossan's previous argument depended on his distinction between literal and metaphorical levels, and since the argument in his counter-criticism of Via makes little or no use of this distinction, one is forced to conclude that he in effect abandoned his argument in its original form. The term "metaphor-story" is nebulous: is it primarily a "metaphor" or a "story," and how are the two entities joined? It may be that one metaphor for the *structure* of the Kingdom of God is, in fact, the structure of Jesus' parabolic system, but one would have to interpret this equivalence ontologically, not semantically or morally.

Inconclusive though Crossan's counter-polemic is, his general view of the story of the Good Samaritan as a parable is, I believe, correct. Patte maintains essentially the same position in somewhat different terms.[14] According to Patte, Jesus did not present an example which the reader could readily duplicate in his own life. The reader is therefore urged not to *act* as the Samaritan did, but to *become* like the Samaritan. Hence, we are dealing with a parable, not an example story. The misinterpretation of the Good Samaritan as an example story started, Patte maintains, with Luke himself, when he presented Jesus as urging the lawyer to "go and do likewise" (Luke 10:37). On account of the cultural gap which separated the Hellenistic Luke from the Palestinian Jesus, the challenging character of the parable was dismissed, and the parable became an example story. But by the use of structural analysis, it is possible to distinguish between Jesus' story, which is an authentic parable, and Luke's presentation of it (Luke 10:25-37), which is an example story.

The analysis leading up to this general conclusion is methodologically Lévi-Straussian in the same sense as Patte's analysis of Galatians I:1-10, with the addition of a number of procedures drawn from the work of Greimas. Implicit in this analysis is the

assumption that three sets of structures impose their constraints upon any simple narrative text:

1. The cultural structures.
2. The structures of the enunciation.
3. The deep structures.

These sets of structures may be further subdivided.

Among the cultural structures are the following:

1. The structures of the specific language used in the text, in this case koinē Greek. Admittedly, the parable was first delivered in Aramaic, but the structuralist exegete has only the Greek text from which to work. He should nevertheless be aware that there may still be constraints of the Aramaic language inherent in the Greek text. The structures of koinē Greek include not only the superficial syntactic structures of the language, but also the paradigmatic structures and the structures of the specific system of signs in koinē Greek. To these structures one should add those dimensions of the generative structure which are strictly cultural: these are, as Chomsky has shown, aspects of generative grammar (and consequently of the generative structure) which belong to the level of deep structures.
2. Those religious, historical, onomastic, geographical, socio-economic, and political structures which are generally termed "cultural codes."
3. The structures of the Jewish literary genre *mashal.*

The structures of the enunciation constitute the constraints imposed upon the discourse by the author and his particular situation in life. To what extent the "author" of the story of the Good Samaritan, in the form which it has come down to us, was Jesus or St. Luke is questionable: structuralists have generally assumed that Jesus was the "author" of the parables, however much they have been altered in oral or written transmission. Among these structures of the enunciation are the following:

1. The structure of the author's argument. In the story of the Good Samaritan Jesus reduced the Jewish literary genre *mashal* to the subgenre "parable," thus producing an inter-

action of a cultural structure and a structure of the enunciation.

2. The constraints of the author's *Sitz im Leben*, as far as they
can now be ascertained. We do not know in which specific
situation Jesus taught this parable: if it was delivered as a
polemic against priests and the levites it would have a connotation different from that if it were delivered as an exhortation
to lawyers to practice charity to their non-Jewish brethren.
Nor do we know the place of the parable in the teaching of
the historical Jesus. St. Luke provides a situation for the
parable itself, but we do not know the circumstances of the
early Hellenistic church (of Corinth?) which led St. Luke to
place the story as he did. If one takes the parable to extend
from Luke 10:25 to 10:37, most of it (10:29-37) would pre-
sumably have had its origin in L.

Among the deep structures are the following:

1. Deep structures of the content, especially the narrative structure, the mythic structure, and the elementary structure.
2. Deep structures of the expression, e.g., the deep phonetic
structures. These are part of structuralist theory, but are not
relevant to the text of the Good Samaritan. They will therefore not be discussed here.

The deep structures are the most difficult to analyze, so some
extra comments on them may be appropriate. Lévi-Strauss called
them "structures of the human mind" or "symbolic functions of
the human mind." Chomsky called them "innate structures,"
while other authors, including Patte, have used the term "archetypal structures." Their importance has been recognized in both
ontology and linguistics.[15] They act as constraints imposed upon
any discourse, but as filters they are semantically empty; hence,
they cannot be equated with Platonic ideas. Models for the deep
structures have been established on the basis of analyses intended
to identify the constants in human communication. These constants are not semantic or phonetic features, but rather the relations which join these features together. As constant relations
they form structures (or substructures) which interact with

each other. These structures are represented by means of algebra-like formulae or abstract models on account of their relational nature. A certain amount of the technical terminology relating to modern theory of deep structures has been devised by Greimas: I use it here since he consciously thought of his work on deep structures as a logical and legitimate development of Lévi-Strauss's thinking on the same subject. It will be relevant to the wider discussion of the methodology of Greimas in Chapter IV.

The narrative structure is best seen as a network of narrative sequences which are related to one another. This type of structure is seen most clearly in narrative texts, but it may also be present in more subtle ways in other kinds of text. There are three types of narrative sequence:

1.   The correlated sequence.
2.   The topical sequence.
3.   The subsequence.

All of these sequences are represented in the story of the Good Samaritan.

The correlated sequences are the initial (explicit) sequence and the final (implicit) sequence. The initial sequence is manifested by the account of a man whose journey is interrupted by robbers and who is deprived by them of both his belongings and of his physical strength. The final sequence, which is not expressed in the Lucan text but which may reasonalby be assumed, is that the man's belongings (or their equivalent) and his strength are eventual-ly returned to him.

The topical sequence is best explained in terms of the fact that a structuralist reading of any narrative presupposes a need to transform an initial situation; i.e., there is a *lack* which must be overcome. The topical sequence, so-called because of its central place in the narrative, explains how the lack is overcome. The topical sequence in the story of the Good Samaritan demonstrates the Samaritan finding a man who *lacks* perfect health, since he is wounded. The Samaritan attempts to overcome this lack: he bandages the man's wounds, bathes them with oil and wine, and then takes him to an inn. Incidentally, two other potential topical

sequences were excluded when the priest and the levite showed no interest in transforming the initial situation or of overcoming the lack which was clearly present.

The subsequence complements the correlated and topical sequences by explaining something about one of the characters which has not yet been made known. To use Propp's terminology and that of some of the other Russian Formalists, if the topical sequence is the "main test," then the subsequences are the "qualifying test" and the "glorifying test."[16] In the story of the Good Samaritan, the part played by the thieves is the subsequence, since it explains how the lack described in the initial correlated sequence came into existence. It is worth noting that this subsequence comes *early* in the story and defines both the opponents of the wounded man and the semantic value of the man himself. The structural hierarchy of the sequences is not necessarily related to the order in which they occur in the text.

The mythic structure is seen most clearly in mythological texts, but may also be seen elsewhere, as in the parables of Jesus. It allows for the apprehension of reality as a meaningful system of reference in contradistinction to the narrative structure which allows for the apprehension of reality as a meaningful process. As an archetypal structure, it imposes upon man a perception of reality in terms of mythemes; as a relational network it organizes these mythemes in a hierarchical manner. The mythic and narrative structures filter the semantic features in two different ways, but they cannot function independently of each other. After all, myths are narratives of a particular kind. Their relationship occurs at the intersection of the mythic and narrative planes.

The oppositions of the mythic structure are oppositions of contraries (e.g., life/death, God/man) not contradictions (life/non-life, God/non-God). The opposition "lack/non-lack" is therefore one of contradictories, and consequently not a part of the mythic structure but of the narrative structure. Louis Marin in the first chapter of his *Sémiotique de la Passion* has in effect argued that the narrative elements which are the opposing terms of the mythic structure are the contents of the two correlated

sequences "lack/non-lack," the mediating term being the content of the topical sequence. Surely this argument is fallacious, since these sequences are contradictories. Patte suggests more convincingly that the oppositon "lack/the semantic value of the hero" is preferable in the case of the mythic structure. "Non-lack" is then the mediating term.

According to Lévi-Strauss, every myth corresponds to his celebrated formula:

$$F_x(a) \; : \; F_y(b) \; :: \; F_x(b) \; : \; F_{\overline{a}}(y)$$

This formula can be read in terms of Lévi-Strauss's original context: "Warfare is to agriculture as predators are to herbivores." Patte applies this formula, with different semantic values, to the mythical structure of the story of the Good Samaritan, and concludes that it can be read: "The truly religious person is to the robbers as the Samaritan is to the wounded man." In other words, the Samaritan is symbolically identified with the truly religious person in the same way that the wounded man is symbolically identified with the robbers. The Samaritan provides a valid mediation between the wounded man and the robbers, while the priest and the levite fail to provide such a mediation. According to the cultural codes, the priest and the levite could reasonably have been expected to provide such a mediation, but in the event they do not.

This application of the Lévi-Straussian formula involves some use of the elementary structure. While not denying the general validity of Patte's identifications, I have reservations about elementary structure theory which lead to the belief that the same identifications could have been made on the basis of a somewhat sounder theoretical substructure than that which is currently employed. As conceived today, the foundation on which elementary structure theory rests is the so-called semiotic square, which utilizes the principles that every semiotic feature has both a contrary and a contradictory, and that between them there is a relation of implication. This semiotic square is in terms of

traditional deductive logic simply Aristotle's Square of Opposition. It is used by structuralists with a credence that sometimes amazes symbolic logicians, who have generally abandoned the Aristotelian Square of Opposition, partly on the grounds that it is not always possible to know whether universal and particular propositions have existential import or not. It has also been attacked on the semantic principle that logical form is a property of sentences rather than of propositions. The confusion that resulted from such criticisms has led to considerable doubt about what is actually meant by contradictories and contraries, especially in relation to their place in elementary structure.

One example of the problem must suffice. An appropriate starting point is the pair of questionable contradictories that appears in several contemporary textbooks on logic:

1. The present King of France is bald.
2. The present King of France is not bald.

Frege argued that these are contradictories; Bertrand Russell argued that they are not. The disagreement arises partly from the question of whether or not contradictoriness is attached to the grammatical form or the logical form of these statements. The grammatical form of a statement is given and observable; the logical form is often hidden by the grammatical form. Although sentences have logical relations to one another, their grammatical structure does not always indicate clearly what the logical relations are. I have argued elsewhere that the logical form of a sentence is the grammatical form that the sentence ought to have, and that the grammatical form is a discernible structural property of that sentence.[17] But as long as confusion exists between logical and grammatical form, there will necessarily be a wide area of disagreement about contradictories and contraries, and consequently over one central aspect of the semiotic square.

Such reservations affect primarily the elementary structure. I have therefore spoken of contradictories and contraries in connection with mythic structure, but on account of misgivings about the validity of the semiotic square, have declined to use them in relation to elementary structure. The theory of elementary

structure needs to be rethought on a logical basis other than that of Aristotle's Square of Opposition. Such a revision, I submit, should be made in terms of symbolic logic. I do not attempt to here, since any such reworking would lead far from the methodology of Lévi-Strauss.

It is perhaps worth mentioning parenthetically that Robert Blanché, the inventor of the so-called "logical hexagon," has also expressed reservations on the validity of the semiotic square.[18] He rightly complained on numerous occasions that the semiotic square is restricted to the conjunction (implication) and the disjunction (opposition) of sentences. If it is to be used for establishing rational universals, all sentences have to be generalized to fit the conjunction or disjunction of their signifying contents. Since modern narrative study utilizes more than two universals, it follows that the semiotic square is inadequate for this reason in addition to the others already mentioned.

There is one aspect of the structures of the enunciation to which I attribute greater importance than does Patte, namely the connotative content derived from Old Testament imagery and rabbinic techniques of teaching. Harald Riesenfeld has argued that the parables of Jesus make use of a repertory of Old Testament images and motifs in a quasi-allegorical way, with the consequence that they are not fully intelligible to anyone not immersed in Old Testament lore. Birger Gerhardsson has applied this argument to the use of the Good Samaritan, maintaining not only that Jesus draws upon Old Testament imagery but also that he employs rabbinic techniques of interpreting this imagery.[19] These views have been much criticized: they clearly run counter to the widely held opinion that the parables are realistic in essence. Gerhardsson has argued specifically that Jesus could have been using the rabbinic rule that a word may be interpreted in its double significance. The Hebrew for "neighbour" is *re'eh*, for "shepherd" *ro'eh*, and both nouns derive from the verb *ra'ah*: on these philological grounds, Gerdhardsson proposed that the original parable may have dealt not with the true neighbour, but with the true shepherd. The lawyer asked the question, "Who

is my neighbour?," and received an answer about the true
shepherd. This wordplay, according to Gerhardsson, is quite in
accord with the techniques of Jewish midrash, as exemplified,
for example, at Qumran.[20]

Gerhardsson may be right, though his contention is perhaps
unprovable. If this supposed shift in meaning really did take place,
it must have occurred before the parable assumed its canonical
form, for the Greek word πλησίον preserves the secondary
interpretation, which accords with the proclivity of the church
for transforming the parables into didactic and paraenetical
vehicles for its own situation: The members of the early Hellenistic church would not need to be reminded of who the true shepherd was, but they would be interested in the lawyer's question.
The secondary meaning would have been secured by the final
imperative: "Go and do likewise."

Here then is further possible corroboration for Patte's proposal
that Jesus preached a parable which the early church (or Luke
himself) turned into an example story. If Gerhardsson's argument
is correct, it cannot but affect the structures of the enunciation,
since it is especially relevant to the semitic philological processes
underlying the Greek text. Nevertheless, any such addition to the
structures of the enunciation would have no effect on the basic
Lévi-Straussian methodology, which is sufficiently flexible to
absorb such augmentations.

Lévi-Strauss's procedures can in a general way also be applied
(with some reservations) to pronouncement pericopes, as Patte has
demonstrated in a comparison of six pronouncements attributed
to Jesus on the subject of entering the Kingdom like a child:
Matt. 18:1-5; Matt. 19:13-15; Mark 10:13-16; Luke 18:15-17;
John 3:1-6; and the Gospel of Thomas 22.[21] Patte here uses an
exegetical rather than a methodological approach, and suggests
that these passages can be compared to the variants of a myth
discussed by Lévi-Strauss. He demonstrates the distinctiveness of
each of the six pericopes, but does not discuss their interrelated-
ness. He explores the distinctive features of temporalization,
spatialization and actorialization in each individual pericope, and

explains through discussion of the narrative syntax and semantic organization of each passage how the connotations of "entering the Kingdom" and "child" vary among these six different cases. Patte's procedure in this investigation is rhetorical and rigorously synchronic. It thus excludes diachronic considerations. The principal conclusion is that the six pericopes reflect distinct kinds of faith, or in other words different systems of convictions within the Christian community as a whole. I would add that since each passage emanated from a different Christian *Sitz im Leben*, it would not be difficult to corroborate Patte's general position with arguments drawn from the geography of early Christianity and its developing theologies. Patte's discussion is, of course, another example of the application to "literate" texts of procedures which have their roots in Lévi-Strauss's methodological thinking. For this reason, one may feel some of the same misgivings as in the case of Leach's analysis of the creation stories in Genesis.

In his later years Lévi-Strauss increasingly spoke as if structuralism had passed out of fashion – as indeed in some respects it had – and resorted less and less frequently to structuralist method. In his posthumously published collection of papers entitled *Le Regard Éloigné* he gives the impression of viewing structuralist methodology with flagging enthusiasm.[22] It is ironic that biblical structuralists were energetically developing his methods and applying them to the text of sacred scripture at the very time when he was starting to think of structuralism as passé. At all events, it is reasonable to conclude that Lévi-Strauss's followers in the field of biblical studies have done more to refine and augment his methodology than he himself could possibly have done during his very full lifetime.

Notes

1. Claude Lévi-Strauss, *Anthropologie Structurale* (Paris: Plon, 1958). The first edition in English, translated by Claire Jacobson and B.G. Schoepf, appeared in 1963 under the title *Structural Anthropology* (New York: Basic Books). The substance of chapter XI had appeared originally in English as an article in *Journal of American Folklore,* Vol. 78 (1955), but it made at first only a relatively small impact. The French version of 1958 exercised a much greater influence, especially among French structuralists. There are thus three versions of chapter XI: one in French (1958) and two in English (1955, 1963). English quotations will be taken from the 1963 version, as being Lévi-Strauss's last approved reworking of the text, though the differences among these three versions are relatively minor matters. The title in both the 1955 and 1963 versions is *The Structural Study of Myth.*
2. Lévi-Strauss, *Structural Anthropology* (New York: Basic Books, 1963), p. 210.
3. *Ibid.,* pp. 211 ff.
4. In *Transactions of the New York Academy of Science,* Vol. 4 (February 1961), Ser. 2, xxiii, pp. 386-96. Essentially the same essay under the title "Genesis as Myth" appears in Edmund Leach, *Genesis as Myth and Other Essays* (London: Jonathan Cape, 1969), pp. 7-24. Quotations in this chapter are taken from the 1969 version. The 1961 text is reprinted in E.N. Hayes and T. Hayes, *Lévi-Strauss: The Anthropologist as Hero* (Cambridge, Mass.: Massachusetts Institute of TechnologyPress, 1970). For Leach's later thinking on biblical mythology see Edmund Leach and Alan Aycock: *Structuralist Interpretations of Biblical Myth* (Cambridge: Cambridge University Press, 1983).
5. Edmund Leach, *Genesis as Myth and Other Essays,* p. 10.
6. The myths in the four volumes of Lévi-Strauss's *Mythologiques* were all taken down by anthropologists working in the field. Their written forms constitute "oral" texts in contradistinction to compositions in writing, which are sometimes referred to as "literate" texts. For a discussion of the theory underlying this distinction see Walter Ong, *Orality and Literacy* (London: Methuen, 1982).
7. See the colloquy with Paul Ricoeur and others under the title "Résponses à quelques questions," in *Ésprit,* Vol. 31 (November 1963), pp. 631 ff. Much the same negative attitude has been expressed by Joseph Blenkinsopp, who observed: "Leach's application of [Lévi-Strauss's] method to biblical material was doomed to failure." See *Soundings,* Vol. 58 (1975), p. 203.
8. Daniel Patte, *What is Structural Exegesis?* (Philadelphia: Fortress Press, 1976), pp. 59-75 and 76-83. Among Patte's later analyses is one of the parable of the Prodigal Son, where he employs a combination of the methods of Lévi-Strauss and A.J. Greimas, in *Semiology and Parables,* ed. Daniel Patte (Pittsburgh: Pickwick Press, 1976), pp. 71-178, and one of Mark 15 and 16 (with Aline Patte) in their *Structural Exegesis: From Theory to Practice* (Philadelphia: Fortress Press, 1978), pp. 39-92. I have not dealt here with these later analyses because they depart to a considerable degree from "pure" Lévi-Straussian theory.
9. Patte, *What is Structural Exegesis?* (Philadelphia: Fortress Press, 1976), p. 60.
10. Patte, *ibid.,* pp. 76-83.
11. Rudolf Bultmann, *The History of the Synoptic Tradition* (New York: Harper & Row, 1963), pp. 177-78. Bultmann's categorization was not based on struc-

turalist principles; it is therefore not considered here. Via's argument is to be found in his article listed *infra* in this paragraph.

12. Louis Marin, "Essai d'analyse structurale d'un récit parabole: Matthieu 13, 1-23," *Études Théologiques et Religieuses,* Vol. 46 (1971), pp. 38-41.

13. *Linguistica Biblica*, Vol. 29/30 (1973), p. 47.

14. Patte, *What is Structural Exegesis?* (Philadelphia: Fortress Press, 1976), p. 83.

15. See B. Oliver, "Depth Grammar as a Methodological Concept in Philosophy," *International Philosophical Quarterly,* Vol. 12 (1972), pp. 111-30, and "The Ontological Structure of Linguistic Theory," *Monist*, Vol. 53 (1969), pp. 262-74; Philip Pettit, "Wittgenstein and the Case for Structuralism," *Journal of the British Society for Phenomenology*, Vol. 3 (1972), pp. 46-57.

16. For some adroit comments on this matter see Fredric Jameson, *The Prison House of Language: A Critical Account of Structuralism and Russian Formalism* (Princeton University Press, 1972), pp. 64-9.

17. David Greenwood, "The Completeness of the Sentenial Calculus," in *Truth and Meaning* (New York: Philosophical Library, 1957), pp. 37-45.

18. Robert Blanché, *Structures Intellectuelles*, 2nd ed. (Paris: J. Vrin, 1969).

19. Harald Riesenfeld, "The Parables in the Synoptic and Johannine Traditions," *Syensk Exegetisk Arsbok*, Vol. 25 (1960), pp. 37-61; Birger Gerhardsson, "The Good Samaritan – The Good Shepherd," *Coniectanea Neotestamentica*, Vol. 16 (1958), pp. 47-63.

20. For support of this view see Krister Stendahl, "The School of St. Matthew and Its Use of the Old Testament," *Acta Seminarii Neotestamentici Upsaliensis*, Vol. 20 (1954), pp. 185 ff; W.H. Brownlee, "Biblical Interpretation Among the Sectaries of the Dead Sea Scrolls," *Biblical Archaeologist*, Vol. 14 (1951), pp. 54-76.

21. Daniel Patte, "Jesus' Pronouncement about Entering the Kingdom Like a Child: A Structural Exegesis," *Semeia*, Vol. 29 (1983), pp. 3-42.

22. Claude Lévi-Strauss, *Le Regard Éloigné* (Paris: Plon, 1984).

The Methodology of Roland Barthes

While deriving much of its content from linguistics, Barthes' methodology developed along quite different lines from that of Lévi-Strauss. His particular form of narrative analysis emerged at the juncture of linguistics, Freudian psychoanalysis, belletristic criticism, and the Marxist understanding of literature as having a predominantly social purpose. His early works, such as *Writing Degree Zero* and *Elements of Semiology,* were formulated in opposition to existentialism, with its emphasis upon subjective individuality, and its indifference towards the role of language in structuring subjectivity. While synchronic in character, his methodology incorporated diachronic elements which are excluded from strictly synchronic literary analyses. There is thus not the sharp antithesis between history and structure in his theory that one finds in the work of Lévi-Strauss and subsequently of A.J. Greimas. I shall refer to Barthes consistently as a structuralist, even though he abandoned structuralism towards the end of his life. In *S/Z* he maintained that, despite his earlier enthusiasm for structuralism, he had realized the uselessness of attempting to develop a satisfactory structuralist methodology for the study of literature. He acknowledged the impossibility of establishing a universal network of relations characteristic of narratives, and finally concluded that the primary role of literature is iconoclastic in relation to the power of language. In this discussion I shall not deal with Barthes' post-structuralist thinking.

As a structuralist, Barthes did not engage in extensive comparative analysis to develop a single structural narrative model. Instead, he probed intensively into the individual text to demonstrate the unique way in which each narrative discloses its meaning through the use of overlapping codes. He contended that narrative, which was his primary field of investigation, was too complex to be reduced to a single paradigmatic model. He was also suspicious of

the so-called "scientific" assumptions involved in these methods.[1] The most fully developed example of his literary methodology was his deep exploration in *S/Z* of the short novella by Balzac, *Sarrasine.*

Barthes is best known among biblical scholars for his structuralist analysis of the story of Jacob's struggle with the angel in Genesis 32:22-32: "*La Lutte avec l'Ange: Analyse Textuelle de Genèse 32:23-33*" in *Analyse Structurale et Exégèse Biblique.*[2] The methodology utilized in this analysis takes for granted the fundamental principles established in *S/Z*, and in Barthes' relatively elementary essay of 1966 entitled "Introduction à L'Analyse structurale des Récits."[3] In the discussion that follows I shall assume that the thinking expressed in these two publications underlies the theory which Barthes uses in his treatment of Genesis 32:22-32.

At the beginning of his analysis, Barthes differentiates his approach from that of the historical-critical scholars by disavowing any scientific or even disciplinary claims for his work. The structural analysis of narrative, he maintains, is not a science or a discipline, but is part of "The newly developing semiology." The purpose of this branch of semiology is to analyse the manner in which a text manifests its meaning rather than to explore the historical process by means of which it was produced as a literary entity. This attitude leads towards the perception of what Barthes describes as the "ineffable individuality" of the text, which he does not subordinate to a general theory of historical development. The ineffable individuality is also referred to by Barthes as the "difference" of the text; i.e., the primal sense of difference which is the point of origin of the author's own sense of individuality, and which is the point of departure and return for the process of his writing. The "difference" is not ultimately reducible to unique literary characteristics, but really is ineffable; this fact arises from the nature of the "paradigm of the difference" of which "each text is the return." In order to appreciate Barthes' theory fully, it will be necessary to examine briefly the Freudian framework which he presupposes.

The natural language is understood as being the product of a "primary symbolization." This is the result, according to Freudian theory, of the prohibition against incest or, as it is often simply called, the Prohibition. In its turn, the Prohibition causes desire, which is deflected towards a "symbolic" object, namely language. Because the initial object of desire is repressed, this "primary symbolization" is not perceived as being symbolic; on the contrary, it is viewed as neutral, constituting a symbolic, homonymic language. But as such it constitutes a negation which separates the sayable from the un-sayable, reflecting the negativity of the Prohibition itself, which separates the desirable from the non-desirable (i.e., that which may not be consciously desired). Lacan developed from this nexus a new understanding of Freud's theory of the unconscious as having the form of speech, i.c., the un-sayable.[4] The "I" is constituted in the moment of the Prohibition as an awareness of difference and separation, and as the "subject" of the Prohibition. The subject constituted in the "forgotten" moment of the Prohibition becomes the conscious "I", the primary symbol of the act of speech, that is to say of the event in which desire is deflected towards a symbolic object, namely language. The "I" thus belongs to this primary level of symbolization, and hence to the primary negativity of language.

Strongly influenced in these matters by both Freud and Lacan, Barthes maintained that the relationship between the subject and the primary symbol is one of desire deflected from its primary object. It therefore follows, according to Barthes, that the act of enunciation to which the "I" refers is the occurrence of this deflected desire. Hence the biological, corporeal force which is operative in this moment effectively gives rise to style, and the necessary force of law that undergirds the unconscious system of language. In Barthes' view writing, especially of a narrative kind, portrays a subject oriented by desire towards symbolic values. The subject reportrays the now "forgotten" event which resulted in the desire directed towards the "symbolic" object, namely lan-guage itself.[5] Hence writing involves a return to the silence of the preverbal state in order to achieve this reportrayal of the primary

process through which the self dramatically emerges as a different-iated, conscious entity. The process of return and reportrayal of differentiation is the "paradigm of the difference" which underlies and produces the structure of the narrative.[6]

Barthes maintained the traditional position that narrative is structured in sentences. He further averred that, however complex it may be, a narrative sentence can be reduced to two basic elements, the subject and the predicate. He thus elaborated on the structure of the narrative sentence: "To narrate (in the classic fashion) is to raise the question as if it were a subject which one delays predicating; and when the predicate (truth) arrives, the sentence, the narrative are over, the world is adjectivized (after we had feared it would not be)."[7] He termed the subject of the narrative the *personnage*, which he understood to be a combination of semes around the same proper name through several different scenes, the distinctive semes constituting the "personal-ity" of the *personnage*.[8] The proper name itself, which serves as a point of semic convergence, is a "field of animation" for these semes; referring virtually to a body, it involves the semic configu-ration in an evolutive, biographical time. The attachment of the semes to a particular name acts as a "blockage" preventing the "reversability" of the text, and limiting the plurality of meanings.[9] It thus fixes the text as a meaningful duration oriented toward the nomination of a single lexematic name.[10]

Behind the name, as a point of unity for a sequence of predi-cates, is the personal voice, which is constituted by a statement or a reference to other statements exhibiting a single recognizable point of view. In Barthes' analysis of *Sarrasine*, the entire text is presented as "a stereographic space where the five codes, the five voices, intersect."[11] The voices represent various fixed points of view or codes which are present in the text: the Voice of Empirics or proairetic code; the Voice of the Person or semic code; the Voice of Science or cultural code; the Voice of Truth or herme-neutic code, and the Voice of Symbol or symbolic code. The textual tissue consists of a series of departures, to listen, so to speak, to these various voices, and repeated returns to the point of

origin which is writing itself. The avenue of these departures is that of connotation.

It is worthwhile emphasizing at this point that Barthes' five codes are neither discrete nor static in the text, nor do they belong only to the text. They are modes of structuralism within whose field the text occurs; they are, in other words, processes rather than prefabricated patterns. As such they do not predict interpretation but only energize, as it were, the process of critical reading. They provide, in one sense, a network of multivalenced signs, the "signifying" of which depends wholly upon the cooperation of the critical reader.

The point of unity for the concourse of five voices in stereographic space is the enigma represented by the undefined name of the subject of the narrative. This enigma is also the fundamental point of departure for narrative structure. In other words, the enigma of the name arises from the mystery which constitutes the origin of the personal voice. This origin is to be found in the "forgotten" event in which the awareness of difference first emerged, i.e., in the Prohibition against incest, the first encounter with the Law.

Barthes' analysis of the text arises from the "paradigm of the difference." Since the paradigm is operative in whatever circumstances narratives are produced, this perspective does not necessarily contradict the historical-critical approach. Barthes indicates that the issue is not one of a methodological confrontation between structural or textual analysis and exegesis.[12] But there is a possible area of conflict in the way in which the final form of the text is to be viewed and used in interpretation. Whereas most commentators see portions of scriptural text as consisting of a patchwork of several earlier sources which must be separated prior to interpretation, Barthes takes the final text as a homogeneous unit. He finds no problem with the possibility that several older and even contradictory sources may still be reflected here. Plurality of meaning, and even contradictions only add to the openness of the text, and thus to its semantic richness.

The basic method which Barthes uses in his textual analysis of

Genesis 32:22-32 is largely derived from that which he developed in *S/Z*. But there are differences, the principal of which is that in his analysis of Jacob's struggle with the angel he makes no use of the cultural, hermeneutic, or symbolic codes. Nevertheless, many of his general comments concerning the unusual ending of the story and the symbolic character of the wound given to Jacob refer to the same phenomena that were treated under the categories of these codes in *S/Z*. His procedure in discussing Jacob's struggle is to analyze the text under two categories, a "Sequential Analysis" and a "Structural Analysis." The latter analysis utilizes concepts derived from Greimas and Propp, partly because their methods are as appropriate to ancient as to modern texts. Barthes' own approach in *S/Z* was patently developed to deal with the complex structures of a relatively modern narrative.

Barthes' use of the functional analysis of Propp demonstrates some degree of methodological adjustment. Since the narrative in Propp's functional analysis must be reduced to fundamental actions, there is a correspondence between certain of his categories (e.g., transfer, combat, marking, victory of the hero, liquidation of lack) and the three sequences which are basic to Barthes' discussion: the Crossing (vv. 22-24), the Struggle (vv. 24-29), and the Namings (vv. 27-32). It should be noted, incidentally, that there is some degree of textual overlap in these sequences. Instead of seeking to reduce the actions to generic categories, as Propp does, Barthes traces their specific sequentiality as it occurs in this particular text, and constructs the sequences on the basis of the units of action found uniquely there. He is thus not attempting to force the text into a preconceived model, but articulating the *actionelle* pattern in such a way as to allow the special meanings of this text to be manifested.

According to Barthes, this passage contains few semes or personal indices. In fact he mentions only two, the references to the strength of Jacob and to his divine election. He introduces his comments on the meaning of Jacob's wound by saying that he is moving in the direction of textual analysis, which he specifies as a "vision *without barriers* of meanings."[13] This definition refers

to meaning which is beyond the syntagmatic structure of the narrative; i.e., symbolic, reversible meaning.

This modification of the approach used in *S/Z* can be understood not only as a consequence of the limited scope of the passage under discussion, but also of Barthes' rather impressionistic approach to the text. His method is not strictly systematic, and is not intended to force the exegete into uniform repetitive modes of analysis in order to achieve the scientific goal of consistency. He does not use methodological notions derived from Greimas or Propp in order to reduce the text to a uniform model. Rather, he uses a few of their techniques to show unusual tensions in the narrative. He denies that he is constructing a scientific method; instead, he maintains that he is in the position of one who is only beginning research, and that his "method" is actually only a "way of proceeding."[14]

Barthes' first procedure is to examine the pattern of the major actions found in the Jacob story, and then to reconstruct the structure of the sequences. This method involves the initial division of the text into its basic sequential units, which he designates as Passage, Struggle and Nomination. Barthes' approach may profitably be compared to that of Gunkel, explained in the Introduction to his edition of Genesis. It was Gunkel's opinion that the myths of Genesis may be divided into scenes.[15] In his analysis of the Penuel myth he found a number of major difficulties in the text. There is the inconsistency between the report in v. 25a that Jacob was injured due to a blow, and in v. 25b as the result of the strain of wrestling; again in vv. 27-28 he is blessed by having a new name given him, whereas in v. 29 he is blessed again following the refusal of the divine assailant to disclose his own name. Then there is the duplication between v. 24, in which the narrator reports the sunrise, and v. 26, in which the assailant reports it. Finally, there is the duplication in the two requests for names — the divine assailant's request for Jacob's name and Jacob's request for the divine name in v. 29.

According to Gunkel, there is a further problem in v. 25, where the antecedent of the pronoun "he" in the clause "he touched the

hollow of his thigh" is unclear if one does not add the concluding clause, "and Jacob's thigh was put out of joint as he wrestled with him." However, as this latter clause appears to be a duplication, the pronominal reference in the original account remains unexplained. A similar ambiguity is found in Hos. 12:4, where the statement "he wept and sought his favour" following a reference to Jacob's struggle could refer either to the angel or to Jacob. This fact led Gunkel to propose that Gen. 32:25a is a fragment from an earlier story in which Jacob defeated the angel by delivering a decisive blow. This fragment, he suggested, was subsequently revised by editors who had abandoned the earlier theology of man as capable of winning in a contest with gods or demons.

There are also parallels which call for consideration at the beginning of the passage. Verse 22 implies that Jacob went across the river, whereas v. 23 indicates that he remained on the north bank. Beginning with these two parallels at the outset of the narratives, Gunkel joined each of them together with the pairs of parallel verses which follow so as to construct two almost complete, and once independent versions of the story. The older version runs from v. 23 to v. 24a, 25a, 26, 27, and 28, originally told of Jacob's remaining on the north bank of the river, triumphing over his assailant, discovering as the morning dawned that the assailant was in some sense divine, and subsequently forcing a blessing from him. Gunkel attributes this version to E because of a parallel to Gen. 30:8 in which the same wrestling figure is used with reference to Rachel's struggle with Leah. The remaining verses, attributed to J, reflect another mentality. They explain that Jacob first crossed the river before meeting his assailant in the night, and then accidentally suffered a dislocated hip as a result of the struggle. The blessing is given in J as a result of Jacob's request for the name of God, whereas in E it is the consequence of the bestowal of a new name.

Barthes' analysis shows obvious similarities to that of Gunkel. In discussing his first sequence, "the Crossing," Barthes finds two parallel series:

I.	rise up v. 22	gather together v. 22	pass over v. 22
II.	gather together v. 23	send over v. 23	remain alone v. 24

Together with Gunkel, Barthes indicates that in v. 22 Jacob crossed the river, whereas in v. 24 he seems to remain alone on the north side. Barthes then proceeds to show how this double beginning leads to a "double reading" of the narrative as a whole:

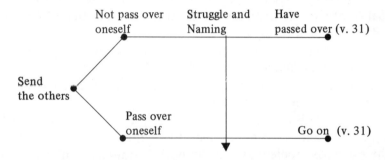

The solitude of Jacob, which Barthes accepts as a part of both readings, has a different connotation in each. His proposal is that Jacob's remaining alone on the *north* bank makes the struggle into a kind of test which he must pass before he can cross, whereas Jacob's struggling on the *south* bank, which was the side of his destination, makes it only a momentary detention in the midst of a passage from one place to another. In the first case his solitude is a preparation for his test, but in the second it is a sign of his separation; i.e., a mark which sets him apart. The first case thus lends itself to a "folkloristic" reading, leading to a name etymology, whereas the second suggests a more anagogical meaning. The passage over the river loses its structural meaning and becomes instead a means of giving a "geographical" air to an occurrence which has no "mythic value." Furthermore, when the struggle is represented only as a detention rather than as a test, the name giving takes on the character of a spiritual rebirth which points more toward the future than to the event which has recently occurred.

Barthes thus detected some of the same narrational tensions as Gunkel, and suggested that the same kind of historical strata may underlie the text; i.e., an older mythological version and a later more theologically mature version. However, rather than separating the two versions on the assumption that the text should have a consistency of religious veiewpoint, he assumed that it was the character of narrative texts to have plural codes and meanings. In fact, he wrote, the textual critic". . . savours such *friction* between two intelligibilities."[16] His attitude towards the conflated quality of Genesis was thus subtly different from that of Gunkel, and indeed of form critics in general. Far from wishing to discover the individual documentary origins of his chosen passage in Genesis, he exhibited a kind of aesthetic delight in the multi-layered nature of the text, and implied that this characteristic was an artistic virtue in itself.

The comparison with Gunkel's method is especially interesting in the next sequence of the narrative, "the Struggle," vv. 24-29. The principal problem as seen by both Barthes and Gunkel is that of the indeterminate reference of the pronouns in v. 25. For Gunkel, the inherent ambiguity is an indication that v. 25a is a fragment of an older version in which Jacob delivered the decisive blow, and that v. 25b is a later version in which this theologically primitive occurence is changed so as to make Jacob the one injured, but only accidentally in the course of the struggle. This particular division of v. 25 leads to the dividing of the concluding verses. The older version leads to Jacob's realization, as day begins to break, that his opponent is a divinity of some kind. Jacob then forces a blessing from him through the bestowal of the new name in vv. 26-28. The later version concludes with Jacob's being overcome by his opponent, while asking for his name but instead receiving a blessing. Thus Gunkel sees the final version of the text as a secondary union of two contradictory versions of this tale, the contradiction itself being without any significance other than an indication of the conservative piety of later editors.

The problem of the unclear pronoun reference is seen by Barthes in a somewhat different way. He perceives in v. 25 the

same ambiguity regarding whether it is Jacob or the assailant who prevails, but he regards this difficulty as being tied to the paradoxical ending of the narrative; i.e., it prepares the reader for the surprising victory of the inferior party. Hence, according to Barthes, the ambiguity should be explained not in terms of the fusion of different versions of the story, but simply as an amphibology which has its own role to play in the structure of the narrative.

Even though he refers to the ambiguity of the reference of the pronouns in 25a ("he prevailed not") and 26 ("And he said, 'Let me go . . .'"), Barthes does not mention the problem of 25b which was crucial for Gunkel ("he touched the hollow of his thigh"). The main problem for Barthes thus does not pertain directly to the matter of who delivered the blow, as it does for Gunkel, but rather to the general lack of clarity of the identity of the partners in the course of the struggle. In contrast to Gunkel, however, it is decisive for Barthes' understanding of the structure that the person who delivers the blow not be the winner in the struggle. The structurally important factor is that the narrative should have a surprise ending. The surprise takes the form of victory for the individual who should under normal circumstances have been the loser in the struggle.

In common with most recent commentators, Barthes took the view that behind the story of Jacob's victory lies a folktale of a man's struggle with a river deity or demon, who had to disappear with the morning light. Hence the paradoxical success of Jacob is in a sense the result of contemporary notions relating to divine-human contact. This fact explains why the narrator would not have revealed the divine identity of the assailant at the outset, since this prior information would have lessened the impact of the unusual ending for hearers or readers who were familiar with such notions. Barthes compares this paradoxical ending, where the inferior, apparently vanquished, party suddenly emerges as the victor, with an endoxical pattern. In this type of pattern, the struggle should have resulted in a deadlock, and then party A would have delivered an unusual blow to party B, thus revealing

his superior technical skill or special knowledge of the art of fighting. Within a normal endoxical narrative logic, such a blow would be decisive and would have given the victory to party A. This particular story, however, continues beyond the conclusive blow, thereby reaching a new stage at which the weaker party can force the stronger party to settle the fight in a negotiation. Victory for the weaker party results.

It is interesting that the pattern is endoxical in both of the earlier versions postulated by Gunkel as underlying the passage. In the older version, according to Gunkel, Jacob won a double victory as a result of delivering the decisive blow to the assailant and then forcing a blessing from him as well. In the later version Jacob is totally vanquished by demon or deity, and at the end knows only the name of his antagonist. This division rests upon the supposed duplication in v. 25, 25a containing reference to Jacob's delivering the blow against the assailant, and 25b referring to the quite different event of the more or less accidental dislocation of Jacob's hip that occurred in the course of the struggle. Gunkel's division assumes inferior stylistic skill on the part of an editor who was far removed in time from the original narratives. This assumption, while not being rejected by biblical scholars in more recent years, no longer commands the same following that it did once. Modern commentators are less inclined than was Gunkel to make assumptions about editorial expertise, or the lack of it. This story may be regarded in stylistic terms as a narrative unity and, if seen from this point of view, lends itself more appropriately to a structuralist treatment.

The interest now being shown in the hermeneutical processes at work in the adaptation of earlier material to the viewpoint of the documentary writers is to a degree a structuralist interest. Whereas Gunkel's larger context of meaning was the documentary hypothesis, Barthes' was that of the structure of the narrative and the semiotic theory which underlies it. He saw the written narrative, rightly or wrongly, as a new secondary language which transcends the natural language, but consists of more or less predicated subjects.

In Barthes' view, the starting point for any system of language as well as for any system of personages in a narrative is a state of unstructured equilibrium. Meaning arises as this equilibrium is unbalanced by the differentiation of one element in relation to another through what linguistis call a "mark." This datum produces the fundamental binary pair
"marked" versus "unmarked."
The kinship system within which the elder/younger brother relationship is defined can be understood from this viewpoint. Barthes holds that at least in theory a state of initial equilibrium exists between an elder and a younger brother in relation to the parents. This equilibrium is disturbed when the elder brother inherits the family's wealth. Thus the older son is "marked" to the disadvantage of the younger "unmarked" son.

Applied to the story of Jacob and Esau, Barthes' theory is that the initial equilibrium was unbalanced when it became clear to Jacob (the younger brother) that Esau (the older brother) would inherit his father's wealth. Jacob, however, acquired this "mark" for himself by cheating Esau out of his birthright. In the story of the nocturnal struggle there is a symbolic reenactment of this drama. The equilibrium presupposed by the beginning of the story is disturbed by the unexpected victory of one of the contestants through the blow to the thigh which partially cripples the other. Through his persistence, however, Jacob also gains a victory. The blow which should have defeated him results in an outer sign, namely the limp, which marks him as having acquired the blessing. There is thus an inversion of the mark, the younger acquiring the inheritance, and the weaker party in the conflict gaining the final victory. Hence, the outer mark of his defeat becomes a sign of triumph. As Barthes explains, the natural order of things has been overturned since, "in this world God marks the young, acts against nature: his (structural) function is to constitute a *counter-marker*.[17] Bearing in mind that the mark is the creator of meaning in the phonology of language, he adds: "By marking Jacob (Israel), God (or the Narrative) permits an anagogical development of meaning, creates the formal operational conditions of a new 'language,'

the election of Israel being its 'message.' God is a logothete, a founder of a new language, and Jacob is here a 'morpheme' of the new language."[18] Thus in his struggle with Esau, Jacob comes to embody the passage from a state of equilibrium to the emergence of a world which, in Barthes' opinion, transcends the predeterminations of the "natural" closed system (of inheritance, law, or language), and opens the possibility of a new "language" to unfold freely beyond all foreclosed meanings from the past.

One may well feel misgivings about Barthes' treatment of his second sequence. The whole notion of initial equilibrium between two brothers being disturbed by the knowledge that one will acquire the patrimony while the other will not seems to assume that jealousy necessarily plays a part in any such relationship. Of course, it may or may not. In the case of Esau and Jacob, the initial suggestion to deceive Isaac came from Rebekah: Jacob himself acted under pressure from his strong-willed mother, and the text gives no evidence of original jealousy on his part. The attempt to show that the "marking" of Jacob is connected with an anagogical development of meaning presupposes the hypothesis that any system of language works similarly to any system of personages in a narrative. That is to say, one must accept as given that words acquire their meanings in a manner analogous to the behavior of characters in literature.

Both of these notions appear to be debatable. The first was clearly influenced by Barthes' sympathy towards Marxist doctrine: it rests on the artificial assumption that equilibrium between two brothers is not disturbed until questions of relative wealth enter their relationship. However, if relationships between siblings are determined primarily by the attitudes and behavior of their parents — as psychologists have often supposed — the fact that Rebekah showed greater favour to Jacob than to Esau would have had a greater effect in unbalancing any such equilibrium. The argument that Jacob's struggle with Esau is somehow analogous to the emergence of a new "language," if seen in the historical context of the Old Testament, is simply not true. It is correct to say that the Hebrews collectively became merged under the name

of Israel, but what "language" ever developed in Israel as a result of the story of Jacob's rivalry with his brother? If the argument is taken in the context of the present day, it seems purely ideological. In either case, Barthes' implied linguistic prophecies are hard to reconcile with the authentic spirit of the biblical story.

Barthes' third sequence is called "The Namings," vv. 27-32. It consists principally of the business about the name. The question concerning the name comes from the adversary first, and subsequently from Jacob. The response is direct on Jacob's part, and indirect on the assailant's part, and the effect in each case is a mutation. Jacob's name is changed to Israel, and the effect of the decision of the deity is to cause a name to be given by Jacob to the place, Penuel. Barthes does not give any independent significance to the blessing which comes in place of the disclosure of the divine name, seeing the benediction formally tied to the nomination in that both are acts of a sovereign. The formal ending of the sequence is not the blessing but Jacob's naming of the place. This nomination Barthes manifests to be structurally parallel to the ending of the previous sequence. Indeed, he finds that all three sequences are structurally homologous, in that all relate in some way or another to a place, a parental line, an alimentary rite, or a personal name.

Barthes' exegesis of the story of Jacob's struggle with the angel demonstrates his methodology clearly. Towards the end of his discussion, he compares his own sequential analysis with the approaches of Propp and Greimas. The primary difference between Barthes, on the one hand, and Propp (followed by Greimas) on the other, is that Propp developed narrative models by collecting and analyzing great numbers of narratives in order to discern their common structural features, whereas Barthes preferred to work in depth with the individual text in order to bring to light the way in which the unique structures of a particular text reveal its own special meanings. This procedure ultimately served his purpose of disclosing the plurality of meanings in a given text.

Incidentally, if one analyzes Genesis 32:22-32 with relation to Greimas's method, in which the interaction among the various

actants in the narrative is reduced to a structural model, one may see, as Barthes makes clear, an overlapping of roles. The actantial narrative pattern of Greimas consists of a subject and object of action, a sender and receiver who transmit and receive the object value with which the action is concerned, and a helper and opponent who support and oppose the subject. Often the subject is also the receiver, as Jacob is in this case, and occasionally the subject may be his own helper as is also the case here, but very rarely is the sender also the opponent, as God appears to be in this situation. He commands Jacob to begin his journey home, and then appears as Jacob's antagonist on the eve of the completion of the journey. This paradoxical overlapping of opposing roles is indeed unusual.

Barthes applied the functional categories of Propp to illuminate the unusual character of this tale, while at the same time showing its close relationship to other folk narratives. Propp had proposed a series of thirty-one "functions" which, he maintained, regularly recur in sequence in the many Russian folk tales he had analyzed.[19] These functions influenced Barthes profoundly and are vitally important for any understanding of Proppian theory. I therefore list them sequentially:

1. One of the members of a family absents himself from home.
2. An interdiction is addressed to the hero.
3. The interdiction is violated.
4. The villain (a new personage) makes an attempt at reconnaissance.
5. The villain receives information about his victim.
6. The villain attempts to deceive his victim in order to take possession of him or of his belongings.
7. The victim submits to deception and thereby unwittingly helps his enemy.
8. The villain causes harm or injury to a member of a family.
9. Misfortune or lack is made known; the hero is approached with a request or command; he is allowed to go or he is dispatched.

10. In those tales in which the hero is a seeker, he agrees to or decides upon counteraction.
11. The hero leaves home.
12. The hero is tested, interrogated, attacked, or otherwise acted upon in such a way as to prepare for his receiving either a magical agent or helper.
13. The hero reacts to the actions of the future donor.
14. The hero acquires the use of a magical agent.
15. Ther hero is transferred, delivered, or led to the whereabouts of an object of search.
16. The hero and the villain join in direct combat.
17. The hero is branded.
18. The villain is defeated.
19. The initial misfortune or lack is liquidated.
20. The hero returns.
21. The hero is pursued.
22. The rescue of the hero from pursuit.
23. The hero, unrecognized, arrives home or in another country.
24. A false hero presents unfounded claims.
25. A difficult task is proposed to the hero.
26. The task is resolved.
27. The hero is recognized.
28. The false hero or villain is exposed.
29. The hero is given a new appearance.
30. The villain is punished.
31. The hero is married and ascends the throne.

It was Barthes' claim that functions 15 to 19 of Propp's categories correspond exactly with the structure of this pericope concerning Jacob. Thus if one begins with function 15, Propp's functions and the Jacob story both have a transfer of the hero from one place to another, a combat between the hero and a villain, the physical (or other) branding of the hero, the victory of the hero, and finally the liquidation of the lack or unhappiness connected with the initial departure of the hero. Barthes found this narrative to be a "veritable stereotype" of the popular account of the difficult passage over a ford guarded by a hostile spirit, a

common type of Russian folk narrative.

Barthes' primary purpose in this procedure was not to prove a congruence between Propp's categories and the structure of Genesis 32:22-32, but to reveal the asyndetic manner in which the elements of the structure are combined. He observed that the themes of the Crossing, the Struggle and the Namings "are *combined*, not 'developed.'"[20] The abbreviated, elliptical style used here in connection with such profound themes led him to describe this passage as a "metonymic montage." The logic of this kind of metonymic style, where words are heavy with unexpressed meaning, where figures are vaguely or symbolically identified, and where profound themes are condensed so drastically that they are only indirectly suggested, was for Barthes the logic of the unconscious. Thus many of the stylistic features which earlier literary critics had attributed to a not especially skillful editor, Barthes saw as evidence of the metonymic logic of the unconscious mind.

Barthes' general approach as evinced in *La Lutte avec l'Ange* prompts two questions:

1. To what extent can the system developed in the analysis of one work be applied to other works?
2. Has Barthes achieved a systematically structuralist approach to the biblical text?

I do not know if there is any answer to the first question. Barthes did not always make use of the same analytical terms in *La Lutte avec l'Ange* as in *S/Z*, and he furthermore applied his earlier method somewhat unevenly. While these inconsistencies may be due to an unwillingness to overload the analysis of such a brief biblical passage with terms which were developed for a much longer analysis of a very different work, the result is that the analysis in *La Lutte* appears more subjective and impressionistic than it really is. However, lack of attention to terminological consistency, with the emphasis being almost totally upon freeing oneself of old language in order to be able to respond to the new character of each work, can indubitably lead to the dissolution of the systematic aspect of analysis, and thus into subjectivity.

With regard to the second question, on the extent to which Barthes developed a systematically structuralist approach to the biblical text, one must insist that, in contrast to the methodologies of "scientific" structuralists, that of Barthes was only partially systematized at best. His aim, however, was not *primarily* to be systematic. Whereas diachronic criticism attempts to determine systematically the authorship of a text and to reconstruct the literary and historical process through which the text was produced as an object, Barthes focused upon the narrative text and the way in which its structure produces meaning. Critics approaching a literary work from a diachronic perspective assume that the provenience of the text is an author writing within the limits of a particular historical period, and that the process of criticism involves the illumination of those objectively discernible forces, economic, political, social or cultic, which find their expression through him. The diachronic determination of the meaning of a text usually involves reconstructing the religious or cultural outlook that permeates the text or that is discernible in the tensions between older and newer literary strata. Language in this context is seen as an instrument for the expression of a given content which can be isolated as the original meaning of the text.

Barthes, on the contrary, made no claim to establish or isolate this original content. Instead, he raised the very different question of the relation of language and writing to the author (or authors) and the subject. Barthes thus strove to explain those fundamental processes through which language shapes the consciousness of authors. He saw narratives as being not only the product of the historical, social setting, but also of the internal mental processes of their writers. His application of the Freudian understanding of language in order to find a basic paradigm for analyzing the texture of narrative took the form of attempting to study a particular text at the beginning of the linguistic process itself. It is, of course undeniable that the pericope which Barthes chose to discuss in *La Lutte avec l'Ange* may or may not have been the work of one author. It has generally been attributed to J, but has also been explained as a conflation of the work of J and E, while

there is no general agreement as to the extent of editorial revision. Furthermore, Barthes analysed not the original Hebrew text but a French translation of it. Nevertheless, these inconvenient matters were, in a sense, irrelevant to his particular methodology, with its limited purposes and semiotic character.

Unscientific though in some ways it is, Barthes' methodology has been instrumental in raising more profound, interdisciplinary questions than that of any other structuralist.[21] This fact may explain at least partially the popularity of his writings at present. He has provided new and penetrating insights into the fundamental character of the biblical narrative. By focusing attention on the subjective element in authorship, he has demonstrated that there are several non-diachronic perspectives to the biblical text which need to be further explored.

Notes

1. See, for example, Roland Barthes, "L'Aventure Semiologique," *Le Monde* (June 1974), p. 28.
2. *Analyse Structurale et Exégèse Biblique* in the *Bibliothèque Théologique* (Neuchâtel: Delachaux et Niestlé, 1971). There are two published English translations of this essay: the earlier in Alfred M. Johnson (trans.), *Structural Analysis and Biblical Exegesis* (Pittsburgh: Pickwick Press, 1974), pp. 21-33, and the later, translated by Stephen Heath, in Roland Barthes, *Image, Music, Text* (New York: Hill and Wang, 1977), pp. 125-141. For his analysis of the story of Jacob's struggle with the angel, Barthes used the French text of the *Bible de Jérusalem*, hence his verse numberings are one ahead of those normally used in English Protestant translations of the Bible. These numberings are retained by Johnson, but silently modified by Heath. I have used Heath's translation for quotations (hence my reference to the pericope as Genesis 32:22-32 in place of Barthes' 32:23-33) and have consistently used the "Protestant" verse numberings. A brief synopsis of this essay is to be found in Sanford Freedman and Carole Taylor, *Roland Barthes: A Bibliographical Reader's Guide* (New York: Garland, 1983), pp. 98 f.
3. Roland Barthes, *S/Z* (Paris: Seuil, 1970); "Introduction à l'Analyse Structurale des Récits," *Communications*, No. 8 (1966), pp. 1-27, English translation by

Stephen Heath in Roland Barthes, *Image, Music, Text* (New York: Hill and Wang, 1977), pp. 79-124.

4. Jacques Lacan, "The Insistence of the Letter in the Unconscious," in *Structuralism*, ed. J. Ehrman (Garden City, New York: Anchor Books, 1966), pp. 101-136.

5. Barthes' earliest statements of this concept were published in 1953 in *Le Degré Zéro de l'Écriture*. The English version, translated by Annette Lavers and Colin Smith appeared in 1967 under the title *Writing Degree Zero* (London: Jonathan Cape), and has since been republished in 1968 (New York: Hill and Wang) and 1970 (Boston: Beacon Press).

6. The French substantive for both "writing" and "scripture" is *écriture*: Barthes uses it regularly in expounding these hypotheses. The English gerund "writing" reflects only inadequately the combination of process and product which underlies the denotation of *écriture*.

7. Roland Barthes, *S/Z*, translated by Richard Miller (New York: Hill and Wang, 1974), p. 76.

8. *Ibid.*, pp. 67 f.

9. *Ibid.*, pp. 29 f.

10. The name has no symbolic value.

11. Roland Barthes, *op. cit. ult.*, p. 21.

12. Roland Barthes, *Image, Music, Text* (New York: Hill and Wang, 1977), p. 127.

13. *Ibid.*, p. 134.

14. *Ibid.*, p. 127.

15. H. Gunkel, *Genesis*, 6th ed. (Gottingen: Vandenhoeck & Ruprecht, 1964), p. xxiv.

16. Roland Barthes, *Image, Music, Text* (New York: Hill and Wang, 1977), p. 131.

17. *Ibid.*, p. 135.

18. *Ibid.*

19. Vladimir Propp, *The Morphology of the Folktale* (Austin: University of Texas Press, 1968).

20. Roland Barthes, *Image, Music, Text* (New York: Hill and Wang, 1977), p. 140.

21. Susan Sontag has called him, perhaps hyperbolically, "the most consistently intelligent, important, and useful critic − stretching that term − to have emerged anywhere in the last fifteen years." This statement was made in 1968. See Susan Sontag's Preface to Roland Barthes, *Writing Degree Zero*, translated by Annette Lavers and Colin Smith (Boston: Beacon Press, 1970), p. xi.

The Methodology of A. J. Greimas

In contrast to the relatively unscientific methodology of Barthes, that of Greimas is consciously and deliberately intended to be scientific. He is a good example of a "deductive" methodologist; i.e., one who brings a model to the text to aid analysis, in contradistinction to an "inductive" methodologist such as Todorov, who prefers to discover a pattern within the text. His basic methodology is set forth in his two books *Sémantique Structurale* and *Du Sens.*[1] In these difficult but seminal works, and elsewhere in his writings, it is clear that his principal aim is to uncover the semantic structures underlying narrative. This is a form of theoretical scientific research, as opposed to the construction of methodologies which can be directly employed in practical application. Greimas is not primarily concerned with the meaning of a text *per se*, but with the semantic structures underlying it. This fact has been overlooked by a number of scholars who, in the past, have complained that long and tedious analyses of literary narratives published by Greimas brought no new insight into their meaning.

Greimas himself has published no structural analysis of biblical narrative, but his methodology has been utilized by several scholars in this field. Patte and Via in particular have combined his methods with those of Lévi-Strauss, with results that have won fairly general acceptance among other structuralist scholars. Louis Marin has combined the methodology of Greimas with that of Jacques Lacan, and demonstrated that the two can be fused.[2] Perhaps the best example of a "pure" application of Greimas's method to scripture is Jean Calloud's analysis of Matthew 4:1-11, the temptation story: it is an important essay which will be discussed later in this chapter.[3]

The principal methodological aim of Greimas is to describe narrative structure in terms of an established linguistic model

derived partly from the Saussurean notion of an underlying *langue* (or competence) which generates a specific *parole* (or perform- ance) and partly from the concept of binary opposition. Greimas argues that our fundamental concepts of "meaning" present them- selves to us through the opposition that we feel exists between basic semes. For example, *dark* is defined in our minds (he claims) principally by our sense of its opposition to *light*, and *up* by its opposition to *down*. This concept of binary oppositions underlies the elementary structure of signification on which the semantic theories of Greimas ultimately rest. Binary oppositions also con- stitute the basis of the deep-lying actantial model, which is the best known feature of his methodology.

The most essential opposition in Greimas's semantics is between "immanence" and "manifestation"; i.e., the opposition between a conceptual map of possible features of the world, independent of any language, and the actual groupings of these features in the words and sentences of a language. The plane of immanence consists of minimal semes which are the result of oppositions (masculine/feminine, old/young, etc.). The lexemes of a particular language manifest certain combinations of these features: the word "woman," for example, combines the semes "female" and "human," which are the result of immanent oppositions. In theory, any semantic structural set requires a hierarchically organized body of semes, but so far no such hierarchy has been constructed. To create one would necessitate an ordered hierarchy of all possible attributes of all possible semes: the creation of such a hierarchy would constitute an enormous task. However, the general law devised by Greimas for a minimum adequacy may be quite simply stated: for any two lexemes that differ in meaning there must be one or more semes which account for that difference.

Since the connotation of a lexeme may vary from one context to another, Greimas postulates that the semantic representation of a lexeme consists of an invariable core (*le noyau sémique*), made up of one or more semes, and a series of contextual semes, each of which will be manifested only in specific contexts. To determine the semantic composition of a particular lexeme, one

should consider all the readings or "sememes" that the lexeme has, and then reduce them to a series of alternative contextual semes. Each of the contextual semes may then be analyzed in relation to its semantic specification.

It is crucial to the methodology of Greimas that correct readings be selected by an actual repetition of semes. He refers to the themes which are repeated in a text as *classemes,* and maintains that they are largely responsible for the coherence of texts. Just as the repetition of semes leads to the formation of classemes, so the repetition of classemes in a text enables the reader to identify the isotopies (i.e., the levels of coherence) which unify it. Once one has identified the various isotopies of a text one can in theory divide a text into its isotopic strata. Greimas has identified what he calls the basic isotopies; the "practical," which is a manifestation of the "cosmological" or the outer world, and the "mythic," which concerns the "noological" or inner world.[4] The example which illustrates this distinction — a *heavy sack* versus a *heavy conscience* — is clear enough, and no doubt the distinction could be made in a large number of cases, especially where two senses of a word are correlated with inner and outer references. But his use of the adjective "mythic" is sometimes different from its use by Lévi-Strauss, who did not have noology in mind when he wrote of "mythic" texts, and the problem is aggravated by the fact that Greimas on occasions uses the term in Lévi-Strauss's normal sense of "connected with myth."

The next stage in Greimas's description is called "normalization." It takes place after the sequences belonging to a single isotopy have been identified. Normalization involves reducing the sentences to a series of subjects and predicates which will be cast in a consistent form so that they can be related to one another. Each sequence is then reduced to a set of nominal phrases (*actants*) and a predicate, the most important element of which is either a verb or a predicate adjective. Predicates may also include modal operators and an adverb or adverbial phrase. Actants may be divided into three opposing pairs:
1. Subject versus Object.

2. Sender (*Destinateur*) versus Receiver (*Destinataire*).
3. Helper (*Adjuvant*) versus Opponent (*Opposant*).

Greimas's intention in this division of actants is to make the structure of the sentence roughly homologous to the plot of a text. The story of a quest, for example, will have a subject and an object, opponents and helpers, and perhaps other actants whose function is to send or receive. Ideally, such a plot might be conceived as an ordered sum of the actantial relations manifested in those sentences which are located on the appropriate isotopy. However, it is clear that one could not simply transcribe sentences in this notation and conflate the results, for the hero will not be the subject of every sentence, nor will other characters necessarily occupy the thematically appropriate actantial roles in all of the sentences. Greimas claims, nevertheless, that his procedure for the normalization of a text helps one "to discover more easily its redundancies and structural articulation."[5]

A further difficulty in Greimasian methodology involves the identification of isotopies: there is no purely objective way in which the limits of isotopies can be precisely established. Greimas has admitted this fact in both *Sémantique Structurale* and *Du Sens.* "The principal difficulty of reading," he comments, "consists in discovering the isotopy of the text and in remaining at that level."[6] Literary theory and semantics face the same problem: "The struggle against the logomachic character of texts, the search for conditions for objectively establishing the isotopies which permit reading, is one of the principal worries of semantic description in its initial phases."[7] In reading a text one gains a sense of what it is about; one isolates a semantic field in which a number of items fall as the topic of the text and hence as the central point of reference to which other items one encounters should, if possible, be related. But, as Greimas himself notes, one can choose at random a series of elements in a text, treat them as a set, and construct some general category encompassing them all: "It is always possible to reduce an inventory, taken on its own, to a constructed sememe."[8] What, then, prevents the reader's activity from being totally arbitrary, though logical? Ideally, the explicit

description of the isotopies of a text should account for all possible coherent readings. But if such a goal is to be even remotely possible, one must formulate some general rules to account for the fact that not every conceivable isotopy is valid for a given text. So far, no *universally valid* conditions for objectively establishing isotopies have been produced, either by Greimas or by any other structuralist.

In Greimas's theory, it should be possible to reduce any text — biblical or otherwise — to a series of sememes and then to show how these sememes combine to form classemes, isotopies, and finally the structured content which is the "global meaning." In fact, however, reduction presupposes the hypothetical representation of structures to be described, but that structuration, in its turn, if it is to be successfully carried out, presupposes a completed reduction. This kind of reciprocal implication is clearly an obstacle to the formulation of a descriptive algorithm, as Greimas understands the term. I would aver that the meaning of a whole is not produced by an objective summing up of the meanings of parts; it is only in the light of hypotheses about the meaning of the whole that the meaning of parts can be defined.

Greimas's methodology also includes the distinction between the deep level of narrativity which is purely logical, and the superficial level, which is anthropomorphic. The deep level is the elementary structural level of the signification, the latter being defined by the presence of two terms and the relationship articulated between them. The deep level is reached in any analysis at the final stage of the deconstruction of the personages, locations, and objects. At this level there takes place the ultimate conversion of the functions into qualifications. According to Greimas narrativity has an achronic basis; indeed, he sees narrativity as the manifestation of an achronic and nonspatial manipulation of semantic contents which are interrelated in fundamental categories of signification. In this respect his conception of narrativity is, in my opinion, superior to that of structuralists who see it simply in terms of synchrony. Nevertheless, it has been criticized, and Claude Bremond has been one of the most significant of

his critics.[9] Bremond regards the Greimasian method as an example of "Platonic nostalgia," and doubts whether Greimas's "biplane" conception of narrativity is applicable to narrative in general.[10] According to Bremond, the essential notion of narrative is obscured by Greimasian methodology. From this negative position Bremond has developed his own logic of narrative in terms of a logic of choices which are possible. However, Bremond's logic of narrative, with its "functions" (i.e., actions and events) which combine into sequences to form a narrative, is not so much a revision of the method of Greimas as a separate methodological system. It has not been widely used in the analysis of biblical texts, and has itself been the subject of a good deal of counter-criticism.[11]

It is very much to the credit of Jean Calloud that he has avoided several of the pitfalls in the theory of Greimas, while retaining a good deal of what is indubitably valid in his methodology. He has demonstrated in his *Structural Analysis of Narrative* that, if the more controversial aspects of Greimas's methodology are for all practical purposes ignored, what remains is adequate for the narrative analysis of scriptural texts. The manner in which Calloud has applied the basic methodology of Greimas is worthy of comment. In *Structural Analysis of Narrative* Calloud provides two exigent and complementary analyses of the temptation story in Matthew 4:1-11, preceded by a relatively elementary treatment of the theory underlying them. The first of the two analyses is narrative or syntactic, dealing with the syntagmatic dimension of discourse, and the second covers the semantic contents of the text. The narrative analysis is based on the principle that narrativity is the manipulation of modalities or the exploitation of transformations. As the first step in this analysis, he uncovers the ordered network of relations governing the combination of meaningful units and imposing constraints upon the interplay of meaning. Hence he constructs a functional and actantial model of the text. This model is essentially a morphosyntactic system involving a number of semantic invariants.

For the purpose of narrative analysis, Calloud divides the text

of Matthew 4:1-11 into sixteen lexies. Having analyzed them, he arrives at several conclusions relating to the functional and actantial schemes of the story of the temptation. Among these are the following:

1. The temptation story includes only functions which belong to the beginning of the syntagmatic model (i.e., the functions necessary for the establishment of the contract between Jesus and the devil).
2. The story exhausts itself in the attempt to establish the *anticontract*, and it does not go further than the *anti-mandating* which is each time refused.
3. The narrative is almost immobile, since it runs in a circle and returns to its starting point at the end. The potential tests remain imaginary and unreal, while the micro-narratives, projected into the future by Satan, are cancelled by reference to the words of the Deuteronomic historian. Hence the positive contract which had been manifested at the time of the baptism of Jesus is here reinforced.
4. The actantial scheme is twofold, involving the questions of the identity of Jesus and the signification of Satan. Jesus figures as the potential anti-subject, but does not invest this position. While Satan cannot invest Jesus in a negative position, he does succeed in investing personages round him in his negative program. These personages serve to bring contradiction and confrontation in the ministry of Jesus.

These initial conclusions should be interpreted as semiotic rather than hermeneutic. The aim of this first analysis was to deal with the signified of the text, especially in relation to compatibility and incompatibility among actantial roles and functions and to the logical succession of the syntagms and sequences. The correlative semantic analysis that follows involves the paradigmatic axis, which is the theoretical locus of all the possible semantic units. Calloud very appropriately deals with the semantic contents in relation to one another, for semes are passed from one semantic unit to another as a result of the parallelism of the isotopies.

Calloud's analysis of the semantic contents of the temptation

story has three weaknesses which have little to do with his use of the methodology of Greimas:

1. This analysis is deficient in formalization; indeed, the results are left quite unformalized.
2. The lexematic level of language has been ignored. No attempt is made to analyze the words in themselves. One result of this lack of a lexical dimension is a tendency towards overgeneralization, which is manifest virtually throughout the analysis. Calloud has instead aimed at describing the semantic values of the prelexematic and metalexematic units. It is only fair to add that he represents the descriptions as part of the afterplay of semantic features in the *reader's* mind. He never represents them as indicating what Jesus or Satan could have thought.
3. Little reference is made to the original Greek text of the story. The text used for analysis is that of the Jerusalem Bible. In fact, both of Calloud's analyses are analyses of a translation. The criticisms made in Chapter II of Edmund Leach's analysis of the Genesis story based solely on the KJV are, in principle, also applicable here.[1][2]

However, this second analysis reveals three valuable structuralist insights relating to Jesus and Satan which are worth special consideration.

1. Jesus's actantial position in the temptation story is not symmetrical to Satan's. Jesus is invested by the Spirit of God in the position of subject for a complex mission which will include the manifestation of his real identity. Satan proposed to him a potential anti-contract. Thus Jesus alone is in the position of subject. It is possible to discover in him all of the relations which can eventually represent the values ascribed to Satan. At the beginning of the story Jesus manifests the positive sign, i.e., the sign of God whose mandate he had accepted. He does not, however, possess this sign as the sender does, or as the anti-sender (Satan) possesses the negative sign. His role as subject establishes him in a position of received positivity and of proposed negativity.
2. The name of Jesus is semiologically complex as used in this

story. Since it unambiguously designates a specific individual, its semantic content is a given provided by an onomastic code. There is no need in this case for semantic deconstruction. Furthermore, the name "Jesus" is semantically empty: because it designates a single individual, it does not contain any of the generic features of a semantic class. It is not defined in the story: it designates and does nothing else. Its coded value represents only a minimal figure common to a series of texts.

3. The position of Satan in the temptation story is consistently that of an anti-sender. His actantial position is defined by his specific relations to the actantial model as a whole, and especially to the positions of the sender (God) and of the sent (Jesus) in the actantial model. Satan is the inverse of God, but this formula cannot be turned round. Clearly, God is not the inverse of Satan. On the semantic axis of hierarchical order, God, Jesus, and Satan are here semantically unequal, though, of course, God and Jesus, as the second person of the Trinity, are equal in terms of historically later theological doctrine.

Subsequent researches of Greimas involved several attempts to construct a typology of cognitive subjects with their corresponding modalities. His expressed intention was to formulate a semiotics of manipulation different from but linked to a semiotics of action.[13] Within the context of this proposed semiotics of manipulation, the manipulation of truth was to be only one particular element of the enunciative act. In the meanwhile, he indicated, we should be able to construct, in the form of simulacra, "*cognitive models found in competence*"[14] capable of accounting for strategies of thought at work in all discourses. It is not easy to see how the principles of such a semiotics of manipulation could be applied directly to scriptural texts without involving at least some of the other drawbacks of Greimas's methodology which have already been discussed.

Nevertheless, it is significant that the first example of the structural analysis of an entire New Testament book is essentially Greimasian, without involving the use of his typology of cognitive subjects. This is the semiotic analysis of the First Epistle of Peter

by Calloud and Genuyt.[15] The methodology used here is in general an application with augmentations of that propounded earlier in Calloud's *Structural Analysis of Narrative*. The authors, however, depend to a noteworthy degree on the theory of the semiotic square. It underlies extensive portions of their analysis, and is logically suspect for the reasons already given in Chapter II. Is it not possible to use the majority of Greimasian procedures without implying the logical validity of the semiotic square?

Notes

1.   A.J. Greimas, *Sémantique Structurale* (Paris: Larousse, 1966); Idem, *Du Sens* (Paris: Seuil, 1970). In both of these works the debt of Greimas to Propp is very apparent; indeed, he took the actantial categories in Propp's *Morphology of the Folktale* as his point of departure in *Sémantique Structurale*. I have not dealt here with Greimas's *Du Sens II*, a collection of papers most of which are concerned primarily with narratology.

2.   See especially Louis Marin's "Essai d'Analyse Structurale d'Actes 10, 1-11, 18," *Recherches de Science Religieuse*, Vol. 58 (1970), pp. 39-61, and his *Sémiotique de la Passion* (Paris: Aubier, Cerf, 1971).

3.   Jean Calloud, *Structural Analysis of Narrative* (Philadelphia: Fortress Press, 1976), pp. 47-108.

4.   Greimas, *Sémantique Structurale*, (Paris: Larousse, 1966), p. 120.

5.   *Ibid.*, p. 158.

6.   *Ibid.*, p. 99.

7.   Greimas, *Du Sens*, (Paris: Seuil, 1970), pp. 93 f.

8.   Greimas, *Sémantique Structurale*, (Paris: Larousse, 1966), p. 167.

9.   See especially Claude Bremond, *Logique de Récit* (Paris: Seuil, 1973).

10.   *Ibid.*, p. 89.

11.   There is a useful discussion of Luke 5:1-11 in terms of the models of Greimas and Bremond in Edgar McKnight, *Meaning in Texts* (Philadelphia: Fortress Press, 1978), pp. 279 ff. It should be compared with the structural analysis of the same pericope by Jean Delorme in his article "Luc V. 1-11: Analyse Structurale et Histoire de la Rédaction" in *New Testament Studies*, Vol. 18 (1972), pp. 331-50. For my review of McKnight's book see *Theological Studies*, Vol. 40 (1979), pp. 178 ff.

12.   There are times when Calloud seems to regard the Greek text as of less importance than the problems raised by his methodology. For example, he comments prior to his narrative analysis: "Our appeal to the Greek text . . . must not constitute

an excuse to avoid the problems raised by the analysis of the chosen version [the Jerusalem Bible]." See *Structural Analysis of Narrative*, p. 48.

13. See, for example, A.J. Greimas and J. Courtès, "The Cognitive Dimension of Narrative Discourse," *New Literary History*, Vol. 7 (1976), pp. 443-447.

14. *Ibid.*, the italics are those of the authors, p. 446.

15. Jean Calloud and François Genuyt, *La Première Épître de Pierre: Analyse Sémiotique* (Paris: Cerf, 1982).

The Methodology of Erhardt Güttemanns

Of the major structuralist scholars working on the text of sacred scripture, Güttgemanns is the only one who has developed a new theology. He calls it generative poetics or linguistic theology, and regards it as a science of texts about God. Basic to his methodology is his concept of text and *Gattung*. Following the lead of Chomsky, he makes a distinction between performance texts and competence texts. The former are those which the competent speaker or hearer has actualized out of the repertoire of possibilities, and biblical texts are among them. Competence texts are those which the competent speaker or hearer has not yet actualized from the repetoire of possibilities, but *could* generate at any time from his language — competence. Hence he envisions three areas for consideration:

1. Texts (performance and competence)
2. *Gattungen*
3. Language-competence.

He asks two questions relating to these areas:

1. From what language-competence are the texts and *Gattungen* generated?
2. In what relationship do the performance texts in the Bible stand to the as yet unrealized competence texts of later interpretation?

According to Güttgemanns, New Testament theology, as generative poetics, has to do exclusively with its sole given. The structural analyst is therefore concerned with texts in their linguisticality, and not with whatever nonlinguistic history lies behind them. The "sense" of a text is not regulated primarily by the givens of history but by the givens of its grammatical basis. Grammar is a system of generative forces which produces both texts and historical acts as distinct manifestations of "sense." The new textual grammar of generative poetics is therefore a theory of generative grammar.[1]

In his article "'Generative Poetik' – Was ist das?" Güttgemanns has provided eight axioms which underlie his theory of generative poetics:

1. A particular text (or sign) is not a result of historical forces but of grammatical forces.
2. The direct object of linguistic analysis is the actuality of a text; the indirect object is the virtuality [*Virtualität*] of grammatical forces.[2]
3. Between the surface of a text and its linguistic basis there is a hierarchical relationship, not a linear relationship of projection or representation, since the sentence is not a syntagmatic expression determined by a particular "sense."
4. Texts can be differentiated by "genres" or "forms"; hence the syntagmatic-paradigmatic structures of a text type represent the matrix of a "sense."[3]
5. Every text (or sign) has a functional character: it follows that generative poetics must therefore include a syntagmatic-pragmatic theory of the hierarchical relationship between the functional character of a text as a whole and the functional character of its parts.
6. Generative and transformational grammar is a branch of game theory.[4]
7. Generative poetics must involve a theory of the expansion of verbal nodes by generative and transformational operations through actants and circumstants.
8. There are several kinds of transformations: syntactic, semantic, and pragmatic, as well as transformation between different languages.[5]

It is, of course, easy to criticize these eight axioms, as well as the sometimes rather nebulous way in which they are formulated and discussed by their originator. I have four principal reservations about them, considered as potential bases for a new theology of the New Testament:

1. They overemphasize the linguistic and semantic characteristics of the New Testament, while underemphasizing its strictly theological content.

2. Like many structuralist principles, they were formulated from an ahistorical perspective.
3. They do not allow for any dependence of the New Testament on the Old Testament.
4. It is debatable whether the books of the New Testament were the result simply of grammatical forces.

However, Güttgemanns is confident that generative poetics will remedy what he calls "the regrettable ghettoizing of tradition-al theology." As a result there will be in the future, he claims, a more cross-disciplinary approach to textual exegesis, especially when rules of transformation as well as rules of generation are applied to the texts themselves. Form critics in the past have been aware of the principal patterns of text-transformations, but have not customarily applied the principles of generative and trans-formational grammar. They will, however, be applied, he avers, in the methodology of generative poetics.

Some light is thrown on the development of these principles in Güttgemanns's *Offene Fragen zur Formgeschichte des Evange-liums*.[6] In this work it becomes clear that the impetus to the inclusion of linguistically-based disciplines arises from Käsemann's emphasis on the theological importance of the narrative mode in the gospels. Against Bultmann and others who saw no essential difference between oral and written transmission, Güttgemanns strongly urges recognition of the uniqueness of the written text.[7] He develops this notion through his concept of gospel as *Gestalt* and in doing so demonstrates that the social matrix and literary entity are not ultimately divisible, but are in fact the horizons of the total linguistic situation.

Once again the influence of Käsemann is apparent in Güttge-manns's article *"Einleitende Bemerkungen zur strukturalen Erzählforschung"* of 1973,[8] where he makes a number of signifi-cant observations on the structural study of narrative, with particular reference to New Testament texts. He starts by succinctly restating Aristotle's theory of narrative as it appears in several places in the *Poetics*, and then proceeds to reformulate it in modern terminology as constituting the foundational position

underlying the modern structuralist understanding of narrative. Aristotelian scholars may well have difficulty in recognizing the concepts of the author of the *Poetics* in Güttgemanns's compressed and rather narrowly technical language, but his reformulation is essentially as follows. The basis of narrative constitutes a coherent structural framework that is conditionally transformable and syntagmatically defined. This structural framework is possible only in terms of actions which are conceivable between an initial situation and a final situation, and which are represented by selected actors. These actors are inserted into the framework by means of what Güttgemanns calls "text-syntagmatic and text-semantic expansions or additions," so that the actions define the actors rather than the character of the actor defining the possible actions. The syntagm of the actions is comprised of three compositional sequences:

1. The initial situation
2. The peripety
3. The final situation.

The various text-types (e.g., tragedy, comedy, etc.) are so generated that compositional sequences are determined with respect to form in terms of *contraries,* but with respect to content in terms of *contradictories.* In comedy (which like most structuralists he sees in both the Old and New Testaments) the syntagmatic movement of the actions runs from an initial disequilibrium, through a mediating peripety, to a final equilibrium. In tragedy (also in both Testaments) the syntagmatic movement of the actions runs from an initial equilibrium, through a mediating peripety, to a final disequilibrium.

In Güttgemanns's opinion, Propp shares with Aristotle the position that in the narrative text-type, the basis is not established by the actors but by their actions; the actors are the variables, while their actions are the invariants or constants. This hypothesis does indeed appear in Propp's *Morphologie des Märchens,* though it is not stated explicitly in Aristotle's *Poetics.* Güttgemanns's ultimate conclusions from these premises are his own, and are technically rather far removed from both Aristotle and Propp.

Broadly, Güttgemanns maintains that narratives must answer to a base grammar of narrative, which itself must comply with the rules of transformational grammar. The nodal points of narrative, the limited repertory of motifemes (narrative actions) and the still more limited repertory of the actants can be structured by means of strict operations of formal logic as a semantically coherent system of terms. This system is capable of producing grammatical rules for narrative syntagmatics.

From these considerations Güttgemanns predicates that the center of narrative textual semantics is the dialectical mediation, and quotes with approval some of Louis Marin's reflections on *médiation,* which he feels are applicable to his own conception of a base-grammar of narrative. Marin at various times has suggested that *récit* (narrative) involves the construction of a mediating operation which attempts to bring together contravalent poles so as to unite disjunctive elements through antinomy.[9] This dialectical alternation neutralizes the disjunction of contraries, so that a *coincidentia oppositorum* results. Hence this dialectic, completed by means of syntactic operations, is at the same time transformation:

In the process of exchange and communication which constitutes narrative in all of the dimensions of its transmission and reception, of its codes and of its expression, there is a transformation in which a transaction [*travail*] between contraries is developed. . . . Such is the referential function in the discourse of the narrative: this function is at one and the same time its condition of existence and the material which the discourse of narrative unceasingly transforms into a product; it struggles with the material relentlessly because this material is not a thing, but a difference among things, not a being, but a difference within being, a productive disjunction.[10]

Ontologically, then, Güttgemanns and Marin are in agreement on how the dialectic of narrative mediation gives to narrative its distinctive manner of being.

This rather abstract theory of narrative is applied to a few pericopes from the synoptic gospels in Güttgemanns's essay *"Narrative Analyse Synoptischer Texte."*[11] By way of introduction,

he reminds his readers that the performance texts (i.e., text surfaces or levels of expression) of the gospels constitute the verbalization of the narrative level of content, and are not to be confused with the narrative itself. While the expression of the sequential ordering is subordinated to time, the content itself obeys only the logic of semantic coherence, for which both its contrary and contradictory oppositions and their complements are simultaneously co-determined. Semantic determination, vocality and isotopy are therefore not representable by the sequential data of the text surface. Consequently, it is not the performance text of a pericope or the totality of its paraphrastic transformations which are to be analyzed, but rather the deep text. By the deep text of a pericope I understand Güttgemanns to mean the underlying semantic content of the narrative, which is independent of the verbalization of natural language, and which remains the same through all translations of the performance text.

Güttgemann's method of analyzing the selected pericopes incorporates four stages:

1. The analyst establishes the particular motifemes which are expressed in the performance texts of the pericopes.
2. The motifemes are written into a matrix which should be applicable to all of the texts which are to be analyzed: this matrix makes it possible to compare the invariants with the narrative constituents, and the variants with the particular text-constituent elements.
3. The semiotic actants are identified.
4. The analyst explains how the text is a transformation of the narrative base.

In applying these stages, Güttgemanns subjects each pericope to two separate analyses, motifemic and actantial.

It would be tedious and repetitive to rehearse the various analyses that Güttgemanns has made for each separate pericope: his procedure is best seen in the pages of his *Narrative Analyse*. These analyses are difficult to criticize in themselves: if one grants Güttgemanns's premises, his analyses are in general logically irrefutable. What is more interesting is his general conclusion from

these analyses, namely that neither the historical Jesus, nor a revealed kerygma is the linguistic basis of synoptic narrative. The linguistic basis is rather the narrative competence of *homoloquens*. The historical Jesus and the revealed kerygma belong, according to Güttgemanns, to the pragmatic basis of narrative proclamation. This basis motivates the proclamation, but simultaneously makes use of an *a priori* linguistic basis. Jesus and the kerygma are therefore a necessary but not sufficient condition for gospel narrative. Rather, the sufficient condition is exclusively the grammatically defined narrative competence of mankind. From this position Güttgemanns arrives at one of his most celebrated pronouncements: grammar ontologically and logically takes precedence over history.

So far this discussion of the methodology of Güttgemanns has not manifested any special insights into pure theology. Indeed, he has stated categorically that traditional New Testament theology is to be rejected, since it is not derived from a textual theory. The basis of his own promised New Testament theology is the linguistic theory underlying generative poetics. This linguistic theory as a foundation for a New Testament theology is discussed by Güttgemanns in *"Linguistisch-literaturwissenschaftliche Grundlegung einer Neutestamentlichen Theologie."*[12]

One cannot avoid being struck (perhaps unpleasantly) by the highly negative and iconoclastic attitude towards other theologies which characterizes Güttgemanns's attitude in this article. This sweeping statement is typical of his outlook: "Everything that has come down to us as the heritage of the fathers appears questionable from the point of view of linguistics: the methods of form criticism and redaction criticism, tradition history and the history of religions, the solution of the synoptic problem and the explanation of the gospel "form," the anthropological lexematics of the presentation of Pauline and Johannine theology, and finally *all* of existential hermeneutics."[13] Basically, Güttgemanns's main complaint is that traditional theology is not a textual science, in contradistinction to generative poetics which is. The enormous advantage of generative poetics over all of its rivals is to be found

in its scientific methodology which is, according to Güttgemanns, "adequate for dealing with the most important problem facing biblical scholars today, namely the analysis of the various biblical text-types."[14] These observations are punctuated by a rather large number of anti-Bultmannian opinions, most of which are concerned with Bultmann's supposed lack of linguistic expertise.

Despite the many protestations of Güttgemanns on the scientific nature of his forthcoming theology, it remains questionable to what extent theology ever will be or could be a science, especially as the element of supernatural faith must always be more or less present in it. I have commented previously on the nature of science:

Science as a whole may be divided into two sub-disciplines: the factual sciences, embracing the totality of all purely empirical disciplines, and the formal sciences, embracing all non-empirical disciplines, of which logic is the corner stone. This difference is based on my belief in the syntactical and semantical dichotomy between analytic and synthetic statements. A statement is analytic if it is unconditionally valid according to the transformation rules which determine under what conditions a statement is a consequence of other statements. Its validity should be independent of the truth or falsity of other statements, and it should be a consequence of the null class of statements. A statement is inconsistent if it is unconditionally invalid, that is, if every statement of the language is a consequence of it. A statement is determinate if it is either analytic or inconsistent, and synthetic if it is neither analytic nor inconsistent. A statement is logical if it contains only logical signs, and descriptive if it contains at least one descriptive sign. While all synthetic statements are descriptive, the converse does not hold good. The range of descriptive sentences is always wider than that of synthetic statements.[15]

Formal sciences, I submit, contain only analytic statements while factual sciences contain only synthetic statements. If theology is to be a science, as Güttgemanns is sure it must be, there is no alternative to its being a formal, not a factual science. As a formal science, its statements ought to be analytic. I am not, however, convinced that all theological statements *could* be analytic, especially those that do not rest on an explicit and analyzable

textual base. The proposition

God is a Trinity of three persons

could not, I maintain, be regarded as an analytic statement in the
context of formal science. Güttgemanns might well argue that this
proposition is scientifically null; for my own part I would argue
that it is not a scientific statement at all. It is the statement of
a doctrine in the context of divine revelation, which cannot be
proved by the application of scientific method any more than it
can be proved by historical method or pure reason. Güttgemanns's
attempt to limit the theological enterprise to a largely linguistic
science is, in my opinion, unreasonably constricting. Theology is
traditionally, and I think correctly, described as *fides quaerens
intellectum*, but Güttgemanns nowhere stipulates that *fides* is
necessary for the practice of generative poetics. It is, I concede, a
worthwhile procedure to apply the principles of scientific linguistics to the text of sacred scripture, but this academic activity is
not in itself theology, nor do I believe that it can constitute a
fully satisfactory foundation for a theology which arises out of
faith.

It should nevertheless be mentioned that the forty-seven basic
methodological rules of generative poetics are assembled in this
particular article more clearly than anywhere else. They are not
arranged in logical order, and there is a certain degree of repetitive-
ness among them. Some are very general in nature, others minutely
specific. I shall therefore discuss only the most fundamental rules
as providing a matrix for the others. It will be noticed that in some
instances they overlap the content of the eight axioms in
"'*Generative Poetik*' – *Was ist das*?" But the purposes of the
eight axioms and those of the forty-seven rules are easily distin-
guishable. Axioms constitute established principles, even if (as in
this case) the establishment is largely limited to the work of one
structuralist author. The rules are broader in scope, and contain a
good deal of non-axiomatic material.

Güttgemanns is especially sensitive in his rules to the difficulties
involved in defining "kerygma." The terms "kerygma" and "kerygmatic" are in his opinion capable of two principal interpretations:

1. They designate a primitive Christian text-type, namely the formulaic sentential statements of primitive Christian proclamation.
2. They designate very generally the authority for all possible impulses toward particular texts, with no precise connection to specific lexemes, periods, or textemes.

The task of the scholar dealing with kerygmatic matters is to restrict his concepts to text-types that can be described in a linguistically non-controvertible manner. In so doing, his entire methodology should be directed toward the linguisticality and textuality of the kerygma. Hence arises rule XVII:

Generative poetics is able to use only such categories and concepts as will adequately provide for the linguisticality and textuality of its object.

Consequently, Güttgemanns's New Testament theology has to do exclusively with the linguisticality and textuality of its scientific object. The constituents of its object are conceived by him as aspects of its textuality.

Rule XIX states:

A New Testament theology built on a linguistic-literary critical basis can only be derived from a general text theory. It is the task of generative poetics to establish such a text theory.

The necessity for such a text theory results from the fact that the "sense" of a text is the result of the methodical application of semantic principles. The lexemes in any text derive their significatory function from a syntagmatic matrix. This principle, according to Güttgemanns, is unrecognized by Bultmann, whose "naive semantics" proceeds from the assumption that words are the carriers of significations, and that "sense" results from the addition and aggregation of these significations. Hence, for Bultmann, lexemes are almost exclusively those linguistic elements that carry objectifiable significations *qua* existentials. To this criticism Bultmann might justifiably have replied that he was not attempting

to compress all New Testament theology into a linguistic mould; thus he identifies the existentials in the New Testament with particular anthropological or theological concepts; e.g., conceptual dualism in Johannine theology.

However, there is a logically deeper division between Güttgemanns and Bultmann: the basic methodological principle of generative poetics is deduction, while that of the historical-critical method is induction. Furthermore, the grammar of this new deductive method must itself be newly created, as is stated in rule IV:

> The text-semantic effect of a text is not to be inferred intuitively from school-grammar; rather it necessitates . . . a text-type transformational grammar. The methodological goal of generative poetics is to create such a grammar.

Most of the rules based on rule IV show the influence of Chomsky's *Syntactic Structures* which had appeared in 1957.[16] They involve the notion that the text-semantic dimension of a text is to be distinguished from its lexeme-semantic dimension, and that semantic levels involve classes of distinctive features that constitute the structure of each level, e.g., phonemes, morphemes, lexemes, syntagms, periodemes, and textemes. Clearly the logic underlying the structures of Güttgemanns's levels is deductive: in this respect he and Bultmann are in different logical categories. I see their methods as complementary rather than antagonistic. They can surely exist together in the same way that deductive and inductive logic exist together.

In rule XXIII Güttgemanns reiterates that the logic of grammar takes precedence over the logic of history. Indeed, in terms of the theory of knowledge, "history" is not a logically or ontologically primary category; the semantic universe is the epistemological *sine qua non* for the recognition of history as history (rule XLV). The author of a text is of no particular concern for generative poetics, except inasmuch as the presence of different authors might demonstrate the presence of different grammars (rule XXV). Traditional exegetical categories like "origins," "gaps" and "overlappings" are unusable in generative poetics, since they cannot be

employed as performance categories (rule XXVI). The term "logic of grammar" should be understood in a generic sense, for there is more than one logic of grammar. Indeed, the texts of the New Testament are constituted on the foundation of two grammars which Güttgemanns calls "basis" grammar and "text" grammar. Of these, "basis grammar" is hierarchically superior. Rule XXXIX applies to the relationship between the two:

> The linguistically persistent preeminence of "basis" grammar over "text" grammar implies that a competent speaker/hearer can possess several grammatical text competencies. These make up the possibilities of "sense," by means of which he can realize performance in grammatically and therefore semantically quite different text types.

Güttgemanns's rather lengthy rule XLVII is virtually a summing up of what he regards is the value of generative poetics. He claims that his new methodology puts an end to the previous lack of contact between grammar and theological thought. The new grammar will be the foundational principle of New Testament theology in the future. As a result, the learning of language and the learning of subject matter will again become the unity which prevailed in what he calls the "*existentiell* theology of primitive Christianity." In his concluding paragraphs he foresees the complete abandonment of Bultmannian existential theology, with its flawed attempt to translate a historical *illic et tunc* to a *hic et nunc* of the present. For this translation to be possible, Güttgemanns maintains that the existentials themselves must be the general anthropological universals which lie at the basis of the *myths* of antiquity. And to express these anthropological universals satisfactorily, transformational grammar and the principles of deductive semantics are essential.

In interpreting Güttgemanns's methodology in general, it would be difficult to overemphasize the importance of his notion of *Gattung,* which is a synonym or functional equivalent of grammar. According to Via, *Gattung* is "the competence which generates a text as one form of expression and not as another. It orders the

linguistic levels (textemes, etc.) and the elements which compose them by selection and arrangement, and it also establishes the relative dominance or hierarchy of the speech functions by selection and combination. Thus in the *Gattung* parable the poetic function predominates, while in theological discourse the metalinguistic (not referential) function is dominant."[17] The precise locus of *Gattung* is, as Via admits, difficult to find. Perhaps it is best to see Güttgemanns's *Gattungen* (or genres) as inherent structures of the human mind, indeterminate in number, which may be conceptually articulated by scientific structural analysis.

But the fact still remains that Güttgemanns places a disproportionate amount of importance on scientific linguistics to the exclusion of virtually every other aspect of biblical interpretation. Scriptural texts can indubitably be analyzed by his methodological procedures, but no amount of scientific theory can fully explain the *inspired* nature of the word of God. Güttgemanns implies in various places that to oppose the principles of generative poetics is to turn the kerygma into referential statements, which refer to something other than themselves. He is to some degree correct: there are many pericopes in the sacred text which are referential statements. But even in the case of Jesus' parables, where the referential function plays only a small part, the inspired nature of the utterances cannot be identified completely with the texts. After all, kergma is not the word of God without a hearer or a reader.

The basic problem, then, is whether any portion of the word of God can properly be analyzed exclusively under the control of a linguistic methodology being operated almost *in vacuo*. Güttgemanns offers no explanation of the element of divine inspiration in the biblical text and, as long as his procedures are based largely on transformational grammar, he is not likely to incorporate explanations of divine inspiration into his methodology.

Furthermore, if the concept of kerygma includes preaching the word of God today, which I believe it does, the inadequacy of generative poetics becomes even more pronounced. I do not think that a kerygmatic sermon, based on the text of scripture and

constituting a genuine language event, can be explained in purely linguistic terms, however technically sophisticated the methodology may be. When one tries to apply Güttgemanns's methodology in these cases, his unacknowledged secularism always gets in the way. In a nutshell, Güttgemanns's system lacks what is so impressive a feature of the hermeneutics of Ernst Fuchs, namely a *Sprachlehre des Glaubens,* a grammar of faith.

Notes

1. See Erhardt Güttgemanns, "'Generative Poetik' – Was ist das? Thesen und Reflexionen zu einer neuen exegetischen Methode," in *Glauben und Grammatik,* ed. Uwe Gerber and E. Güttgemanns (Bonn: Verlag Linguistica Biblica, 1973), pp. 153 ff.
2. This and the following axiom show an indubitable dependence on the work of Noam Chomsky, and especially on his distinction between the surface (or performance) of a text and its deep structure (or competence). See in particular his "Deep Structure, Surface Structure, and Semantic Interpretation" in *Semantics: An Interdisciplinary Reader in Philosophy, Linguistics, and Psychology,* eds. Dan Steinberg and Leon Jakobovits (New York: Cambridge University Press, 1971). The province of generative and transformational rules is to be found between the surface of a text and its grammatical basis.
3. Applied to the gospels, this axiom predicates that the macrosyntactic structure is the matrix of the "sense" or significatory function of each gospel.
4. This axiom is clearly based on the analogy between language and chess made by Ludwig Wittgenstein in his *Tractatus Logico-Philosophicus.*
5. This latter type of transformation principally concerns translation; Güttgemanns suggests that it calls for a theory of semantic universals.
6. Erhardt Güttgemanns, *Offene Fragen zur Formgeschichte des Evangeliums,* 2d ed. (Munich: Chr. Kaiser Verlag, 1971). The English translation by William G. Doty appeared under the title *Candid Questions Concerning Gospel Form Criticism* (Pittsburgh: Pickwick Press, 1979). It contains a number of additons by the author, who also composed an Epilogue to the English translation. I have treated it very briefly here because it is not a work in the context of structuralism. It does, however, provide some of the linguistic concepts which the author later developed much more fully in his generative poetics.
7. A similar regard for the text as such is to be found in Paul Ricoeur's article, "The Problem of the Double-Sense as Hermeneutic Problem and as Semantic Problem,

in *Myths and Symbols,* ed. J.M. Kitagawa and C.H. Long (Chicago: University of Chicago Press, 1969), pp. 63-79.

8. Erhardt Güttgemanns, *"Einleitende Bemerkungen zur strukturalen Erzahlforschung," Linguistica Biblica*, Vol. 23/24 (1973), pp. 2-47.
9. See, for example, Louis Marin, *Sémiotique de la Passion* (Paris: Aubier, 1971), pp. 9 ff. The ideas in the remainder of this paragraph are ultimately derived from this source, pp. 10-14, but Güttgemanns does, in effect, make them his own.
10. Marin, *Sémiotique de la Passion*, p. 13.
11. Erhardt Güttgemanns, *"Narrative Analyse Synoptischer Texte," Linguistica Biblica*, Vol. 25/26 (1973), pp. 50-73.
12. Erhardt Güttgemanns, *"Linguistisch-literaturwissenschaftliche Grundlegung einer Neutestamentlichen Theologie," Linguistica Biblica*, Vol. 13/14 (1972), pp. 2-18. Hereafter, this article is referred to as *"Grundlegung."*
13. Güttgemanns, *"Grundlegung,"* p. 17. One is immediately reminded of Erich Grässer's earlier reaction to Güttgemanns's "linguistic attack against the entire New Testament guild." See *Wissenschaft und Praxis*, Vol. 60 (1971), p. 38.
14. Güttgemanns, *"Grundlegung,"* p. 16.
15. David Greenwood, *The Nature of Science* (New York: Kennikat Press, 1971), pp. 2 f.
16. Noam Chomsky, *Syntactic Structures* (The Hague: Mouton, 1957). I also see in Güttgemanns's generative poetics concepts which are derived directly or indirectly from J.J. Katz and Paul Postal, *An Integrated Theory of Linguistic Descriptions* (Cambridge: Massachusetts Institute of Technology Press, 1964).
17. Dan Via, *Kerygma and Comedy in the New Testament* (Philadelphia: Fortress Press, 1975), p. 24.

6

Other Structuralist Methodologies

The work of four structuralists will be discussed in this chapter: Chabrol, Starobinski, Marin and Via. Their methodologies are not strictly original, but rather develop or combine already existing methodologies with some degree of originality. To these discussions I have added some reflections on the typology of signs of Umberto Eco, who is a semiotician in a broad sense rather than a structuralist, but whose thinking on semiotic analysis has a certain amount in common with that of structuralists in the field of biblical studies, and has exerted some influence on them. It will be noted that I have not included any observations on the methodology of Michel Foucault, who — whatever some writers claim — denied being a structuralist, on the ground that a linguistic model cannot be used for the study of any system of symbolic values that characterizes a culture.

The methodology of Claude Chabrol incorporates elements drawn from the work of Lévi-Strauss, Greimas and Barthes. However, his conception of meaning (*sens*) differs somewhat from that of Barthes: he does not recognize Barthes' "hidden signified," and replaces it with a "hidden signifier," which is for all practical purposes a network of correlations. For Chabrol, meaning "is not *behind* the text; it is the system of rules which permits one to generate the differential interplay of oppositions which controls my reading of the length of an 'infinite' text of which the text I read is only a contingent and limited — which is to say historical — actualization."[1]

Chabrol's essay "Analyse du 'Texte' de la Passion" provides a fairly typical example of the application of his methodology.[2] He takes the three synoptic passion narratives as variants of one metatext, and compares them first among themselves, and secondly to the Peter and Cornelius episode in Acts. He then sets out to establish the "semantic universe which underlies the text."

However, the analysis of the text of the three synoptic passion narratives is cursory: the comparative content is actually greater than the analytical. The models of Lévi-Strauss and Greimas are both utilized, but in such an incomplete manner that they could easily be reduced to the functioning of one homologous structure. Chabrol sees Jesus as neither ritually pure nor ritually impure, but in a state of what he calls "communal indifferentiation." Unfortunately this position is not, in my opinion, explicable on the basis of his structural anaysis.

There are three general disadvantages of Chabrol's methodology as it is employed in his "*Analyse du 'Texte' de la Passion*":

1. The hypothetical concept of a synoptic "metatext" situated in the context of a supposed "infinite" text is a quasi-metaphysical notion, since neither the "metatext" nor the "infinite" text has any real existence. Conclusions relating to the semantic universe underlying the biblical text may be of questionable value when they necessarily involve such supposititious entities.[3]

2. The combination of methodological notions derived from Barthes with the models of Lévi-Strauss and Greimas is not entirely successful. The models cannot be justified in terms of Barthesian methodology, and are applied in a manner which would probably not have satisfied either Lévi-Strauss or Greimas.

3. Chabrol's use of the French language is far from lucid. Indeed, of all the French structuralists, he is among the most obscure. One of his most trying characteristics is his use of pronouns with no one clearly identifiable antecedent; another is his tendency to use neologisms without defining them. Hence whole stretches of his polemic are sometimes difficult or impossible to grasp with exactitude.

Jean Starobinski is another structuralist whose methodology is in some respects comparable to that of Barthes, but whose presentation is considerably clearer than that of Chabrol. A good example of his work is to be found in his article "The Struggle with Legion: A Literary Analysis of Mark 5:1-20."[4] He explains

at the beginning that this is a purely *literary* reading: like Barthes, Starobinski makes no claim to be engaged in any kind of scientific activity. But his article evinces a structuralist reading: he analyzes the text in its synchrony, and makes no attempt to situate it within the context of historic time. A structuralist analysis he observes, "concerns itself with all the elements of the text as homogeneous givens."[5]

The primary characteristic of the Markan text, according to Starobinski, is that it is anonymous: though attributed to Mark, the text itself gives no indication of authorship. The author is referred to by Starobinski as the "narrator whose person is absent." The effacement of the narrator as subject, he argues, works in favor of emphasizing Christ as the one who uses the first person: the narrator speaks only to make others speak, without even attributing to himself the role of witness. Nevertheless, the narrator does attribute to himself knowledge of the identity of all the personages who intervene in his narrative. He also knows that Christ is the Son of God, and consequently is able to distinguish between those who have seen the truth and those who have not. This opposition carries the implication that those who refused to believe in Christ must be guilty of some form of culpable blindness. Hence, Starobinski maintains, the text gives birth to a reading in which a valid judgment on the activities of the actors immediately invites faith. In other words, the assent which accompanies every reading made in the authentic spirit of the Markan gospel is "imperceptibly changed into an act of belief which, going *beyond that which is written,* is borne toward *the one of whom it is written.* The text is structured in such a way that the reader (or hearer) of the Gospel is made of a disciple of Christ, *ipso facto,* by the interposed narrative."[6]

Starobinski notes that the text does not mention any explicit audience. The absence of an audience, he writes, has the effect of universalizing the recipient. Christ's message reaches the reader not only because his words are sufficiently general to surpass the circumstances which provoked them, but also because the general circumstances are of a kind that the readers can symbolically apply to themselves.

The hero of the story is Jesus himself, described by Starobinski in structuralist terms as "the immutable representative of the singular."[7] He cannot be the equal of anyone with whom he associates: his role as master and healer commits him to a perpetually asymetrical relationship most often indicated by a singular/plural opposition. Starobinski sees the relationship between Jesus and the demoniac as being initially one between two individuals who realize each other's uniqueness. But this relationship is very temporary, and finishes when the demoniac says "My name is Legion." On the other hand, Starobinski adds, "the absence of the *numerical* indication of the singular/plural opposition is compensated for by the accentuation of the *qualitative* indication of the Good/Evil opposition, or Son of God/Demon."[8] The oppositional structure thus remains intact. Jesus, then, addresses himself to plurality, but his efficacious intervention is to a considerable degree singularistic.

Starobinski's analysis of "The Struggle with Legion" demonstrates clearly the opposition between the unchanging singularity of Jesus and the process of the demoniac's pluralization. Nonstructuralist exegetes might well reply that this aspect of the story is not its most important, either in theological or literary terms. Such a reply would be to a degree justified. But structuralist methods are well suited to bringing out some aspects of biblical stories which have been neglected in the past, and if one views this particular pericope solely in a structuralist context, its mutual oppositions are especially striking. In 5:2 a man appears "possessed by an unclean spirit." Starobinski notes that there is a double singular (man, spirit) here. When the man in 5:7 prostrates himself before Jesus, speaks to him, and begs him, the man still speaks in the singular, "What is there between you and me, Jesus, son of the Most-High God? I beg you in the name of God; do not torment me." It is, of course, a very ambiguous singular in which both a man and a demon can speak. The supplication is addressed to Christ, who is the clearly designated addressee, but the speaker does not make himself clearly known. The use of the first person singular produces a degree of grammatical ambiguity: the same

subject, ἐμοί is used to cover the denotations of the man and of the demons within him. In response, Jesus reprimands the unclean spirit in the singular, as if he temporarily ignored its plural nature: "Come out of this man, unclean spirit" (5:8). And again, giving him a singular nature, Jesus asks his name: "What is your name?," Τί ὄνομά σοι; (5:9). The demon himself had instantly recognized Christ and greeted him as Son of the Most-High God. The demonic powers − because they are spiritual beings − instantly recognize the identity of Jesus, their mortal enemy. The name that the demon surrenders to Jesus is a collective singular: "Legion is my name," Λεγιὼν ὄνομά μοι (5:9). Starobinski explains that the term *legion* is rich in easily revealed implications and connotations. It designates hostile troops, the Roman invader, and perhaps even those who will crucify Christ. From now on the plural can proliferate: "because we are many," Ὅτι πολλοί ἐσμέν (5:9). The same voice which said, "My name" (Ὄνομά μοι), immediately says "we are" (ἐσμέν). It has become a collective voice. A syntactic cleavage brings a new (plural) subject out of the preceding (singular) subject. However, in 5:10 once again there is an oscillation between the singular and the plural: "And *he* begged him insistently not to send *them* out of the country," Καὶ παρεκάλει αὐτὸν πολλὰ ἵνα μὴ αὐτὰ ἀποστείλη ἔξω τῆς χώρας.

The phrase which follows (5:11) unexpectedly produces a new collective singular ("the herd," ἀγέλη), but its complement ("of swine," χοίρων) immediately gives rise to the plurality. In the second use of the verb "to beg" (παρεκάλεσαν) in 5:12, the subject is definitely in the plural. Finally the subject appears completely in a nominal and verbal plural quality: "And the unclean spirits came out" or Καὶ ἐξελθόντα τὰ πνεύμοιτα τὰ ἀκάθαρτα (5:13). The expulsion of the evil powers takes place in stages in which the external objectification is emphasized. The name is surrendered, and the progressive pluralization is now an issue forced out of the person of the possessed man. The entry of the demons into the bodies of the animals and their fall into the sea will only complete the movement of externalization, giving to the deliverance its quasi-hyperbolic expression. The departure of the demons from

the man is completed by their entry into another host. The pre-fixes are loaded with a rudimentary but strong value, indicating the crossing of a boundary towards the outside (ἐκ) or towards the inside (εἰς). At the end of the process of deliverance, a triple crossing will take place: out of the man, into the bodies of the swine, and *into the sea* (5:13).

Starobinski investigates comprehensively several other opposi-tions; e.g., the state of possession/the state of healing and Jesus recognized/Jesus rejected. His method is essentially the same in these investigations as in his analysis of the singularity of Jesus/ pluralization of the demoniac opposition. Towards the end of his analysis he attempts, less successfully, to apply the parabolic code to the text. However, the story of the struggle with Legion is clearly not a parable: this part of Starobinski's analysis is strained by his attempt to see parabolic significance in what is presented textually as a historic miracle story.

Structuralist methodologies extend from the strictly scientific to the purely literary, with the majority incorporating concepts that are both scientific and artistic. Starobinski's methodology, like that of Barthes, is a good example of one that is purely literary: it is noteworthy for its comparative lack of scientific terminology and for its greater emphasis on such matters as oppositions, the parabolic code, syntactical structure, and the different levels of semantic connotation. Above all, Starobinski understands clearly what some structuralists do not, namely that structuralist methodology almost incorporates some degree of circularity. He expresses this fact well: "What is to be under-stood becomes that which permits understanding; what permits interpretation becomes that which must be interpreted."[9] This principle underlies scientific structuralist methodologies as much as their literary counterparts.

The methodology of Louis Marin is, as has already been observ-ed, largely a combination of the methodologies of Greimas and Jacques Lacan, with some original features which assist in forming a fairly satisfactory synthesis. The influence of Lacan explains the strong interest that Marin shows in psychiatric theories of the

structure of the unconscious. Much of his work is concerned with the psychology of communication as represented in the biblical text. Marin's most exhaustive and sophisticated contribution to structuralism as applied to the biblical text is his *Sémiotique de la Passion*, published in Paris in 1971. However, his basic methodology is more easily explicable in relation to two of his essays which were published in *Languages,* Vol. 22 (1971), and have since been issued in English under the titles "The Women at the Tomb" and "Jesus before Pilate."[10]

Marin's textual analysis in "The Women at the Tomb" is largely founded on Greimas's actantial model. The general model devised by Marin for the passion of Jesus in both "The Women at the Tomb" and "Jesus before Pilate" may be diagrammed thus:

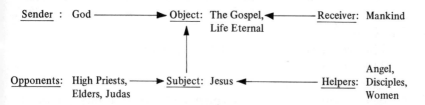

When the women come to the tomb, their actantial object is the body of the crucified Jesus; in place of the object they find a youth wearing a white robe (in Mark), an angel (in Matthew), two men in dazzling garments (in Luke), or two angels in white (in John), all of whom bear the same message: Jesus is risen. The relationship between the women and Jesus himself is a passive and subjective one; their primary concern is the dead body of Jesus.

In terms of the actantial model, one may make the following observations:

1. The angel (angels, youth or men) possesses the *helper* status, but he is also a *mediator* between the sender (God) and the receiver (mankind).
2. The *opponent actant* is the priests, the elders, and Judas considered as a collective singular.

3. The *object actant* is the good news of eternal life.

In terms of the functions of the story, Marin comments that the basic narrative is "well organized as a micro-test," by which he means that a definite lack exists at the beginning, but is liquidated at the end. This liquidation, he observes, is not effective but only virtual, since it takes place solely in the form of a verbal message which is not generally believed.

Marin's analysis of the text is based primarily on Matthew's narrative, with portions of other parallel narratives being used as variants. He points out that not all the oppositions in the story of the women at the tomb occur in all the evangelists' accounts of it. Thus the light/darkness opposition is especially evident in the Johannine narrative, but is not present in Mark. Other oppositions are present in all the accounts: the most important are life/death and individual/society. Matthew's narrative itself is analyzed in four sections:

1. The arrival of the women at the sepulchre
2. The arrival of the angel
3. The angel's discourse
4. The departure of the women and the transmission of the angel's message.

In Section (3) the angel's discourse is further divided into three segments, thus:

1st segment: "I know that you seek Jesus Christ, who was crucified; he is not here." This is an affirmation which is accompanied by its counter-proof: "See the place where he lay," which Marin transcribes symbolically as

$$\underline{q} + \underline{p}$$

where q = quest and p = presence.

2nd segment: "He has been raised from the dead as he said." Marin calls this segment a "discourse in the second degree," since it recalls a previous discourse of Christ announcing his resurrection. This previous discourse predicts Christ's non-presence, represented symbolically as

$$\overline{p}$$

3rd segment: "Come and see the place where he was laid, and then go quickly and tell his disciples: 'He has been raised from the dead, and is going on before you into Galilee; there you will see him.' That is what I tell you." This third segment repeats the discourse in the second degree, but it here becomes a message. Marin transcribes it symbolically as

$$\overline{p} + \overline{q} \, ,$$

meaning that the quest is repudiated by its satisfaction.
The division of the passage and the symbolism are Marin's own, though one is throughout this analysis aware of the underlying actantial model of Greimas.

Marin's analysis of the story of the women at the tomb manifests his subtlety and technical sophistication, but at the same time exhibits what is perhaps the principal weakness of his method, namely that in it the *kerygma* becomes merely a kind of epiphenomenon of the structural features of the story. Hence this account appears in Marin's treatment of it to be a metacommunication about communications, and is not presented as having anything existentially meaningful in it. The system of transformations from model to model which displays the underlying structure *is* the meaning. The "plot" is simply ignored, as also are the dramatic existential potentialities displayed by the narrative. Instead, Marin seems to be engaged in a kind of *miroitement du sens* (the phrase is his own). He sees the story almost entirely as a surface narrative dealing with communications, which display analyzable structures and substructures.

Much the same general comments could be made of Marin's analysis of the story of Jesus before Pilate. The basic text is Matthew 27:1-2, 11-31, and the corresponding texts in Mark and Luke are regarded as arbitrary variants. Perhaps the methodologically most distinctive portion of this analysis is that dealing with the problem of the minimal sequential unit. Not all structuralists

define a sequence in the same way, but for Marin the minimal sequential unit is "the *process* indicated by a verb or its equivalent."[11] Thus the following pericope contains three sequential units:

And after having bound him, they led him away and delivered him to the governor Pilate.

The three sequential units are:
1. And after having bound him
2. they led him away
3. they delivered him to the governor Pilate.

It should be noted that in this type of analysis subordinate clauses are just as much sequential units as main clauses.

The limits of a sequence should be fixed, according to Marin, in terms of the *closure of a process.* Thus in the case of the sequence here given, a portion of the passion story is described from one particular point of departure (the palace of Caiphas) to one particular point of arrival (the palace of Pilate). Marin predicates that the action of binding Jesus is strictly part of the previous sequence: it may be considered connotatively in the present sequence only to the extent to which the person is "delivered as an object." One may consider the sequence ended "when the object is transferred at the end of the movement, since its end (in the teleological and temporal sense of the term) is indeed this delivery."[12] It would be unfair to criticize this position, since the problem involved is largely one of definition. However, one should be aware that other structuralists have somewhat different conceptions of the structural sequence.

Marin's *Sémiotique de la Passion* manifests his rather logocentric methology in its most highly developed form. Considerable importance is attached in this work to the construction of toponymic systems, an area in which Marin demonstrates a noteworthy degree of originality. There are times when he can also display what to some semanticists may appear to be mere hair splitting. Thus he regards as a "fundamental problem" the question of whether the toponym "Mount of Olives" is a true proper name, since the words "mount" and "olives" are both common nouns. In

Appendix III he suggests a highly ingenious solution to the problem, but one is left wondering to what extent the problem was artificial in the first place. In some respects Marin's polemic is almost neo-scholastic in character, but he has contributed to structuralist theory a degree of logical refinement which is probably without parallel.

Dan Via's methodology is eclectic: one is conscious of principles drawn from a number of structuralist writers, especially Barthes, Greimas, Claude Bremond, and to a lesser extent Güttgemanns. One of his most interesting investigations has been that of three Pauline texts with a view to demonstrating a structural relationship between St. Paul's theology of the death and resurrection of Jesus, and the death and resurrection image in ancient Greek religion which gave birth to comedy.[13] Proceeding along structuralist lines, he makes no effort to establish a causal-genetic relationship between St. Paul's theology and either Hellenistic religions or ancient Greek religion, but rather a structural-generic relationship between the death-resurrection motif in St. Paul's writings and that same motif which lies behind classical Greek comedy. The three Pauline texts used by Via are I Corinthians 1:18 – 2:5; Romans 9:30 – 10:21; and Romans 4. On the basis of these texts, Via maintains that Paul's writings in general belong to the comic genre.[14]

One of the Principles on which Via's argument rests is that while *myth* is dominant in tragedy, it is *logos* that is most prominent in comedy.[15] In I Cor. 1:18-31 the power of the word replaces the resurrection, hence the binary opposition cross/resurrection is replaced by the formula cross/word. The resurrection is thus seen as the power of the word. Indeed, the word subsequently functions even more widely in the passage as both the power of God and the resurrected Christ, in addition to the fact that God and Christ are experienced through the word. These concepts all constitute part of what Via regards as the comic structure of St. Paul's thinking.

Another part of Via's basic argument is derived from the theories of Francis Cornford.[16] The essence of Cornford's

historical position was that Greek Comedy (as in Aristophanes) emerged from folk drama, which itself developed from an ancient fertility ritual. This prototypal ritual included the performance of some kind of marriage ceremony intended to enhance the fertility of the land, and in some cases the enactment of the death of an old king followed by his resurrection and restoration. The fundamental structure of Aristophanic comedy, according to Cornford, may be arranged schematically thus:

1. The hero in the agon (the first episode) engages in a struggle with an antagonist and wins a victory.
2. He offers a sacrifice and participates in a feast to celebrate his victory.
3. He then leads a *komos* (victory procession), enters into some kind of marriage, and finally experiences a resurrection of some sort.

The hero is often an *eiron* who pretends to be less wise than he really is; he is usually contrasted with the *alazon*, a boastful pretender who claims an undeserved share in the victory. The plot contains no element of romantic love, so nothing in the plot accounts for the appearance of the woman at the end, who is to be married to the hero. Cornford explains her role as a survival from the ancient fertility ritual. He thereby unwittingly followed the generally accepted structuralist principle that when an element cannot be accounted for at the syntagmatic level, it is best explained by recourse to the paradigm.

Via sees a definite similarity between Cornford's explanation of classical Greek comedy and St. Paul's views on the resurrected Christ. There are, he maintains, two classical comic motifs at work in I Cor: 18-31. These are:

1. The victory of the free son over the guilty father.
2. The victory of the *eiron* over the *alazon.*

God identifies himself with the humble — the crucified Christ and the church — and is thus the *eiron* in this particular literary context. Likewise the world is the *alazon.* Via explains the merging of the two motifs thus:

The alazon is shown that his wisdom is really a foolish illusion (that he can dispose of his own existence); therefore, the crushing of the guilty son turns out to be the crushing of his existence in illusion and self-deception, and he is really thereby freed for life and wisdom. The irony of God is that he enters into (he saves through the foolish kerygma) the suffering and humiliation (the cross) caused by man's illusion (that he runs the world) and thereby shatters that illusion. But God's victory, which is the defeat of the alazon-world, ironically is the victory of man as freedom for new life. Thus the eiron—hero—God does not simply win a victory for himself over the alazon and chase the latter away. While man prior to being brought to naught by the eiron—God was a combination of the guilty son of tragedy and the alazon of comedy, after his "defeat" he is the free son of comedy, but a son who is reconciled to rather than victorious over his father.[17]

On the basis of this and comparable explanations, Via regularly uses the term "Pauline comedy" in relation to the Pauline writings, and claims that the New Testament kerygma as a whole belongs to the structure of comedy.

Perhaps Via may be reading too much Cornford into St. Paul's epistles. It is debatable whether St. Paul would have regarded himself as a writer in the comic genre. Methodologically, Via's approach is not programmatically structuralist; he does utilize phenomenological and existentialist modes of interpretation in addition to his basically structuralist rationale. But there is no doubt that death and resurrection are both inherent in St. Paul's kerygma as well as lying at the origins of Greek comedy. Even if Via's attempt to depict St. Paul as a comic writer has not so far drawn any large following, his principal arguments are hard to deny on *purely structuralist grounds.* Whatever shortcomings are present in his reasoning would appear to be the results of the limitations of structuralism itself.

Umberto Eco is known chiefly as a semiotician.[18] His typology of signs is both original and flexible, though sometimes lacking in clarity. One of the peculiar features of his semiotics is his concept of an "aesthetic idiolect," a special language peculiar to literary art, which induces in readers a sense of "cosmicity," i.e., of endlessly moving beyond each established level of meaning the moment it is established, and of continuously transforming its

denotations into new connotations. Literary art appears to Eco as a way of connecting "aesthetic messages" together so as to produce "texts" in which the "rule-breaking" roles of ambiguity and self-reference are fostered and organized. The connecting process involves four principles:

1. Many messages on different levels should be ambiguously organized.
2. The ambiguities should follow a precise design.
3. Both the normal and ambiguous devices in any one message should exert a contextual pressure on the normal and ambiguous devices in all the others.
4. The way in which the rules of one system are violated by one message should be the same as that in which the rules of other systems are violated by their messages.

This process has some similarities to the one described by Barthes in his account of myth, where what has been established as a *sign* on one level of signification can be "drained" so that it can then become a *signifier* on another level. It also confirms Barthes' account of connotation as a "second order" system of signification based upon denotation.

The concept of aesthetic messages was applied by Eco in *Le Forme del Contenuto* to the question of the language hypothetically spoken in the Garden of Eden by Adam and Eve.[19] His purpose was not philological — he was not interested in their natural language — but semiotic; namely, to discover whether there is a way of generating aesthetic messages in an Edenic language. He first explains that for an aesthetic message to come into being, it is not enough to establish ambiguity at the level of the form of the content. There must also be alterations in the form in which the message is expressed, and these alterations must be significant enough to require the recipient of the message, though aware of a change in the form of content, to refer back to the message itself as a physical entity. He or she can thus detect alterations in the form of its expression. Eco then sets up a number of connotative chains based on a very simple vocabulary, and discusses their use in connection with the events leading up to

and including the committing of the first sin of disobedience and the expulsion from Eden.

For the present purpose, the theory underlying Edenic language is not directly significant: it is a branch of pure semiotic, and its relationship to the text of scripture is peripheral. But Eco's discussion of the matter makes it clear that aesthetic messages can be generated in an Edenic language: any future application of the notion of aesthetic idiolect to the biblical text could be affected, if only obliquely, by this conclusion.

Notes

1.   Claude Chabrol, "Problèmes de la Sémiotique Narrative des Récits Bibliques," *Langages* Vol. 22 (June 1971), p. 8.
2.   Claude Chabrol, "Analyse du 'Texte' de la Passion," *Langages* Vol. 22 (June 1971), pp. 75-96. An English translation appears in Alfred M. Johnson, ed., *The New Testament and Structuralism* (Pittsburgh: The Pickwick Press, 1976), pp. 145-185.
3.   In this respect Chabrol's methodology is to a degree ontological in nature, without having any explicit foundations in ontology.
4.   Jean Starobinski, "The Struggle with Legion: A Literary Analysis of Mark 5:1-20," *New Literary History*, Vol. 4 (1973), pp. 331-56. I have consistently used this English version of Starobinski's article. The original French text appeared in the collection of interpretational essays entitled *Analyse Structurale et Exégèse Biblique* (Neuchâtel: Delachaux et Niestlé, 1971). The translation in *New Literary History* by Dan Via differs slightly from the original, but not in essentials. Two other English translations have appeared with minor differences between them: "An Essay in Literary Analysis – Mark 5:1-20," in *The Ecumenical Review*, Vol. 23 (1971), pp. 377-397, and in Alfred M. Johnson (trans.), *Structural Analysis and Biblical Exegesis* (Pittsburgh: The Pickwick Press, 1974), pp. 57-84. Johnson discusses the problems of the three different translations of this article in his Translator's Preface.
5.   *Ibid.*, p. 332.
6.   *Ibid.*, p. 335.
7.   *Ibid.*, p. 341.
8.   *Ibid.*
9.   *Ibid.*, p. 355.
10. Louis Marin, *Sémiotique de la Passion* (Paris: Aubier, Cerf, 1971); translated into

English by Alfred M. Johnson under the title *The Semiotics of the Passion Narrative* (Pittsburgh: Pickwick Press, 1980). The two essays under discussion are translated into English in Alfred M. Johnson (ed.), *The New Testament and Structuralism* (Pittsburgh: Pickwick Press, 1976), pp. 73-144. I have consistently quoted from the English translations of these two essays.

11. Alfred M. Johnson (ed.), *The New Testament and Structuralism* (Pittsburgh: Pickwick Press, 1976), p. 123. (The italics are mine.)
12. *Ibid.*, p. 124.
13. Dan Via, *Kerygma and Comedy in the New Testament* (Philadelphia: Fortress Press, 1975), pp. 39-69.
14. The word "comic" is used by Via in the classical sense, and does not, of course, mean "funny" or "laughable."
15. Dan Via, *op. cit.*, p. 41.
16. See especially Francis Cornford, *The origin of Attic Comedy* (Cambridge: Cambridge University Press, 1934).
17. Dan Via, *op. cit.*, p. 48.
18. Umberto Eco's work *A Theory of Semiotics* (Bloomington: Indiana University Press, 1976) has been one of his most influential. For an interesting comparison between Eco's approach to structural exegesis in this book and that of Greimas and Courtès in their comprehensive *Sémiotique Dictionnaire Raisonné de la Théorie du Langage* see Daniel Patte's article "One Text: Several Structures" in *Semeia*, Vol. 18 (1980), pp. 9 ff.
19. Umberto Eco, *Le Forme del Contenuto* (Milan: Bompiani, 1971). The model for Eco's Edenic language was borrowed from George Miller's Grammarama project as described in his *Psychology and Communication* (New York: Basic Books, 1967). An Edemic language is an artificial and symbolic one intended to be universally comprehensible.

An Assessment of Structural Analysis

Much of the vagueness which at present surrounds the term "structuralism" is apparent from the methodologies which have been discussed. Structural methods may be scientific, quasi-scientific, or unscientific; they may also be objective or subjective or involve both characteristics in varying degrees. The manner in which these methods are presented is sometimes a source of obfuscation rather than enlightenment. Structuralists have not been generally distinguished for the clarity of their style: obscurities, clumsiness, nebulosity, awkward neologisms and sheer gracelessness are all too common features of their theoretical disquisitions. Even the standard expressions of structuralism sometimes have different meanings for different authors; for example, the terms "code," "message," and "sequence" do not carry the same denotations in the works of Lévi-Strauss, Jakobson and Greimas, quite apart from their use by structuralists trained in communications engineering, cybernetics, proxemics and computer theory.

Additional problems arise when the hypotheses of structuralism are applied to the biblical text. Many of these problems arise from the fact that the principles of structural analysis were never intended by their original devisers to be applied to sacred scripture: it has already been remarked in Chapter II that Lévi-Strauss had considerable reservations about the application of his own methodology to the early chapters of Genesis, and that Paul Ricoeur shared with him a comparably negative attitude. Though Saussure's work marks the beginning of structural linguistics, the historical origin of the structural analysis of narrative is Propp's *Morphology of the Folktale*, a work which underlies a good deal of later analytical theory. It was first published in Russian in 1928, at the end of the formalist period; however, it did not appear in French until 1965. This fact explains at least partially

why so many French structuralists writing in the fifties and the early sixties of the present century derived their notions of Propp's narrative analysis at second hand, and sometimes with a certain degree of imprecision.[1]

There is no evidence whatever that Propp conceived of his methodology as being applicable to the Bible: his primary interest was the morphology of the Russian folktales, a definitely secular genre. His intentions were ambitious; Paul Ricoeur once remarked that Propp wanted to become "the Linnaeus of folklore." As far as Propp himself had a model, it was the classificatory method used by Goethe in his botanical writings. Propp's general aim was to describe Russian folktales according to their constitutive parts, and to investigate the relationship of these parts to one another. Discovering that the same actions are found in several folktales, but that these actions are attibuted to different characters, Propp decided to use these actions (or *functions* as he called them) to isolate a matrix which would permit one to define the structure of every tale. His matrix consisted of thirty-one functions, a rather large number which was subsequently reduced by Greimas in his modifications of Propp's methodology. But on the basis of this matrix, Propp maintained that the entire set of folktales which he was studying could be considered as a chain of variants produced from a single model, and numerous structuralists have followed him in this matter.

The disadvantages of this type of method when applied to the text of scripture may be briefly summarized:

1. Propp isolated his matrix syntagmatically on the basis of evidence derived initially from one hundred folk or fairy tales, and maintained that the succession of the functions was always identical. The same evidence is not available to the biblical scholar, since the number of what can indubitably be called folktales in the Bible is so small, and they are themselves so relatively brief, that literary generalizations based on them are almost automatically suspect.

2. Propp maintained that the constant elements of the folktale are the functions of the characters: this premise is not true of

the undoubted biblical folktales of the Bible considered collectively. The reason is that the biblical folktales cannot be .regarded in the Proppian manner as a chain of variants produced from a single model.

3. It is debatable whether some stories in the Bible are folktales or not. Most scholars would agree that the stories associated with Samson give every impression of being folktales, but what of the accounts of Ruth and Jonah? Should these be regarded as folktales or novellas?

4. The notion, still sometimes encountered, that Propp's functions have a universal validity is simply not true: they are not appropriate to the Icelandic saga, for example, nor to many of those sets of folk stories which are connected with creation mythology. Propp himself conceded that his analytical methods were not suitable for the folktales of Grimm and Anderson, or for "artificially created folktales."

5. The Russian folktale and the biblical folk story were intended for different audiences and were transmitted for very dissimilar purposes.

To these general disadvantages of Proppian method, I would add the further one that it leads to special difficulties when applied to the biblical parables. Parables are *not* folktales. They are not related to one another as are the various folktales within a folkloristic corpus. It would be impossible to demonstrate paradigmatically that the parables of the Old Testament and of Jesus overlie a basic biblical parable in the same way that Propp claims all Russian folktales as constituting variable actualizations of *the* basic Russian folktale. In fact, there is no basic biblical parable at all, still less is there one in Propp's "form," ruled by a rigid concatenation of an irreversible order of functions. The "form" of which Propp speaks, i.e., the matrix of thirty-one functions, is actually not even part of the deep structure, but is an artifact of the surface structure.

The fact that some of Propp's methods have been used by French structuralists in ways which he could not have foreseen and might well have criticized is partly the result of the semiotic

differences between formalism and structuralism. It was Shklovsky who commented that Russian formalism and French structuralism are related as uncle to nephew; perhaps a better analogy might be crossed cousins within an endogamous kinship system. They are related by their dependence on Saussure's foundational distinction between *langue* and *parole,* and on the difference between synchrony and diachrony which lies behind it. However, their practitioners have exploited the distinction in different ways. The formalists were ultimately concerned with the way in which the individual text (or *parole*) was perceived differentially against the background of the literary system as a whole (or *langue*). The structuralists on the other hand, have set themselves the tasks of rewriting the grammar, syntax, and semiology of the total sign-system, and of applying their results, in varying stages of incompleteness, to individual texts. This fact helps to explain the considerable emphasis in modern structuralist theory on the philosophy of models, a feature which has no precise methodological counterpart in Russian formalism.

The work of Propp has been to some degree eclipsed by that of Lévi-Strauss, who gave the theory of myth an importance in structuralist problematics which it has never lost. Since structural anthropologists and biblical theologians use the term "myth" in somewhat different ways, it may be helpful to clarify the differences between structuralist and theological understandings of the word. According to Lévi-Strauss, who was heavily influenced by the Hegelian logic of thesis, antithesis, and synthesis, the structure of myth is dialectical. Within it, opposed logical positions are stated, the oppositions mediated by a restatement, which again, when its internal structure becomes clear, gives rise to another kind of opposition, which in its turn is mediated or resolved, and so on indefinitely. On the assumption that it is the *nature* of myth to mediate contradictions, the method of analysis must proceed by distinguishing the oppositions and the mediating elements. The *function* of myth is to portray the contradictions in the basic premises of the culture. Hence *myth* may be loosely defined in the Lévi-Straussian conception of it as a contemplation

of the more or less unsatisfactory compromises which are part of the life of any community. In the veiled statements of a myth people can recognize indirectly what it would be difficult to admit openly. The relationship of myth to social reality is dialectical, in this view, like the structure of myth itself. And in terms of the significance of mythology, Lévi-Strauss maintained that mythological thinking is a homologue of all thinking.

Biblical scholars in general see myth less anthropologically and, with a few exceptions, outside the context of the Hegelian dialectic. One of the best known recent treatments of myth in theology is that of Professor Maurice Wiles in *The Myth of God Incarnate*.[2] He explains that the use of the word "myth" in English is less than 150 years old, and that its place in theology was established principally as a result of the discussions following the publication in 1846 of George Eliot's translation of Strauss's *Das Leben Jesu, kritisch bearbeitet*.[3] The debate on the matter flourished again with particular intensity in the demythologizing controversy precipitated by Bultmann's essay of 1941, *Offenbarung und Heilsgeschehen*. Wiles recognizes four basic Christian myths:
1. The creation story
2. The fall story
3. Christ's incarnation and work of atonement
4. The corporeal resurrection of the dead and the last judgment.
He explains that these myths are not true or false in the sense that testable scientific hypotheses are true or false. Like poetry, myths can be interpreted at a variety of different levels and can have more than one legitimate interpretation even at the same level. Wiles does not provide his own definition of myth, but he does aver that a myth must contain "some ontological truth corresponding to the central characteristics of the structure of the myth."[4]

I perceive this element of ontological truth as the primary and basic difference between "myth" in theology and "myth" in structuralist theory, as derived from Propp and Lévi-Strauss. This is not to say that the structuralist denies the existence of ontological truth in theological myth: what he does in practice is to ignore

it. Those structuralists who have analyzed portions of the biblical text have not so far regarded ontological truth as an area of analysis. The absence of methodological procedures for the evaluation of ontological truth constitutes a serious deficiency in relation to biblical mythology, though it is, of course, irrelevant to the kind of myths that Propp and Lévi-Strauss analyzed.

The problem of the analysis of ontological truth in biblical mythology is closely tied to another problem in contemporary structuralism, namely that of the possibility of a purely inductive method of structural analysis. I shall argue that purely inductive structural analysis is *not* possible, and that consequently inductivists can claim only that their methods are more or less inductive.

In support of this general hypothesis, the following considerations are relevant:

1. In the area of structural linguistics, the non-inductive nature of language study is generally accepted; Emmon Bach and Jean Piaget have both been consistently emphatic on this subject. Hence it is not surprising to find that the models relating to linguistic structural analyses are often self-consciously deductive in nature.[5] Raymond Boudon has gone as far as to suggest that most literary structuralists are engaged not in a scientific but in a "magical" pursuit, and that attempts to show that structuralism is (or can be) an inductive science are bound to fail. In this connection it is illuminating to recall Sir Karl Popper's classic argument that a theory of induction has no place even in the logic of science.[6]

2. Inductivists engaged in language analysis generally presuppose a hierarchy of domains. This hierarchichal view, however, assumes that in language analysis some structures (e.g., phonological) are more objective than other structures (e.g., semantic), an assumption that may or may not be true. "Structure," as an abstract, hypothetical construct, does not lend itself to this type of hierarchical division, especially when the hierarchy is ideologically tilted in favour of a merely presumed objectivity.

3. There is no scientific procedure for assessing the meaning-value

of such matters as style or connotation. The attempts of some scholars in the field of stylostatistics to apply inductive methods to the analysis of scripture have not been notably successful.[7] The special weakness of this type of approach is that it rests on the a priori assumption that every biblical author had his own particular "style," a hypothesis which is sometimes extended to a school of writers, e.g., those in the Deuteronomic or Priestly traditions. But one may reasonably question whether every author's "style" is necessarily recognizable, especially after an undeterminable amount of editorial revision. Furthermore, the books of some authors (e.g., Obadiah, Jude) are so short that hypotheses on their style derived from frequency-distributions and distinctiveness-ratios can hardly carry much conviction, especially as it is never possible in the nature of this kind of textual criticism to determine the mathematical frequency of verbal or stylistic coincidences. This fact is especially true where random sampling methods are used: the possible margin of error must always be enormous. Historians of English literature will remember that stylostatistics have been used to "prove" that the works generally credited to Shakespeare were actually written by Lord Bacon: few literary scholars take these arguments seriously nowadays.

4. The imposition of hypotheses derived from statistical methods applied to the biblical text is to some extent analogous to the attempts that used to be made by some musicologists – and now happily abandoned – to determine the authorship of anonymous pieces of late medieval music by juggling mathematically with aggregations of supposed contrapuntal and harmonic peculiarities. Literary style, like musical style, is an extension of the author's (or composer's) personality. The extent to which personality can be analyzed by computation is essentially the extent to which the stylostatistical method in scriptural studies is of value.

5. The inductive approach to textual analysis relegates all exegesis that is not based on phonemic and grammatical investigations

to the area of the arbitrary and the subjective. Hence, for the inductivist, textual analysis should be objective not only in its initial phases of *identifying* units of a language corpus, but also in its phase of *describing* the patterns encompassing the relationships of these units. But in fact such objectivity is not possible. Segmentation of the text into lexies, an essential preliminary stage in many types of structural analysis, is to a considerable degree personal, and sometimes purely arbitrary. This situation will probably continue: there is no formal procedure whereby such segmentation may be scientifically accomplished. Furthermore, phonemes are often hypothetical constructs, as also are such content-units as sememes and mythemes. In short, there is no purely inductive method for identifying units of a language corpus or of describing the relationship patterns among these units. This is not to say that some kind of method is undesirable, but it does indicate that structural analysis will always incorporate, in whatever method used, some degree of subjectivism and intuition.

From these general considerations, I conclude that there can be no such thing as a purely inductive structuralist methodology. Certainly some methodologies can be more inductive than others; no one would deny that those of Todorov and Greimas utilize more inductive polemic than those of Barthes and Starobinski, but it remains true that even the most inductive of structuralist methodologists necessarily incorporate a certain degree of non-inductive reasoning into their analyses, even if they do not admit to doing so.

Structuralist methods as applied to the biblical text are most convincing when they are seen in the context of semiotics rather than of inductive logic. If one accepts this position, it follows that any structural analysis of sacred scripture will manifest the strengths and weaknesses of semiotic procedures in general. To be interpreted semiotically, structural analyses of the biblical text should normally be formulated at the intersection of four sign-systems:

1. A sign-system comprising a *signifier* (its expression plane) and

a *signified* (its content plane).
2. A sign-system consisting collectively of the text studied and the structural analysis itself.
3. A sign-system combining a model (viewed as the *signifier*) and the structures (viewed as the *signified of the analysis*).
4. The text being studied, conceived as a language product and therefore already a sign-system. [In terms of (2) the text is a sign-subsystem.]

Structural analysis as sign may be viewed in its dual role as the meaning or content of an object, and the expression of a subject. But in either case the results of any structural analysis should not be seen as examples of pure exegesis or as manifesting a new form of hermeneutic. Structuralism can aid both exegesis and hermeneutics to a degree, but it is still ancillary to both of them.

To what extent, then, do structuralist methods aid exegesis and hermeneutics? The answer to this question depends, it seems to me, on how such methods are applied. Structuralism becomes a *cul-de-sac* once it treats the kerygmatic content of the Bible as subordinate to the underlying structures of the text.[8] The constant tendency in virtually all structuralist methodologies is to render the structures and the codes of greater significance than the message which they bear. One remedy for this rather infelicitious state of affairs is to place more emphasis on surface-structures and less on deep-structures. Another is to divide structural analysis from structural ideology. The first of these possible remedies presents no special technical problems, but the second calls for some historical comment.

It is undeniable that the ideology of structuralism is for the most part Hegelian. This fact is due largely to the influence of Hegel on Lévi-Strauss and through him on Greimas. But is adapted Hegelian dialectic really necessary for a valid interpretation of portions of the biblical text? It may be helpful in those cases where the notion of thesis – antithesis – synthesis is appropriate, but it is in fact not vital to the linguistic aspects of structuralism, nor is it well suited to harmonize with many of the particular problems of biblical theology. Historically, structuralist ideology

developed separately from structuralist semiotics. The two can be separated, and I suggest they should be, leaving structuralism as a *primarily* semiotic enterprise.

If this point of view is accepted, it follows that the structural analysis of texts should be regarded as incorporating the sign theory of language. This factor indubitably constitutes a difficulty, since there is a certain amount of opposition among hermeneutical scholars and biblical theologians to the sign theory. Perhaps the most widely read critic of this theory today is Hans Gadamer, who has taken Heidegger's theory of understanding, and evolved from it a speculative hermeneutics that is language-centered and ontological in character. Fundamental to Gadamer's conception is the rejection of the sign theory. To see words as signs, he feels, is to rob them of their primordial power and to make them mere instruments or designators. In his work *Truth and Method* he traces the conception of the sign theory in Western thought from the idea of *logos* in ancient Greece, through the notions of mathematical symbolism evolved by Leibnitz, to present day thinking on the subject.[9] He concludes that a word is not merely a sign, and that language is something other than a sign system.

The difference between Gadamer's view of language and that of most structuralists is essentially the difference between the linguistic conceptions of Heidegger and Saussure. For Gadamer, language is always fluid and never fixed; indeed, the movement of living language is constantly operating against the fixity of dogmatic statements in general. Saussure, while realizing that language is evolutionary, and that the nature of the sign is to some degree arbitrary, aimed at setting up the foundational principles of a formal linguistic system. Necessarily his view of language is more static than that of the speculative philosopher who is not primarily concerned with linguistic description. Gadamer is, of course, right when he argues that a word is not merely a sign: one could argue against any grammarian that the word "apple" is not merely a noun. However, for purposes of categorization the description "noun" as applied to an apple is denotatively convenient. The sign theory provides a systematic concept of language which

underlies virtually all modern semiotics: it also is convenient, though no structuralist would claim that it fully explains those fluid and connotative aspects of language which Gadamer has in mind.

Structuralism, utilizing the sign system with its admitted limitations, can aid exegesis and hermeneutics principally in two ways:

1. Structuralism provides a set of related methodologies of text analysis to complement such older procedures as form criticism, redaction criticism and rhetorical criticism. Structuralism cannot replace these older procedures, but it can bring a new light to bear on semiotic aspects of the text which have heretofore been generally unobserved. Seing the biblical text in terms of sequences (or strings), syntagms, oppositions, and transformations does bring a new meaning to it, even if that meaning may, in some instances, appear to some degree artificially contrived. Historical, cultural, and conceptual factors must all be taken into account when the analyst is attempting to determine the transformations within a set or structure: these factors inevitably affect the interpretative process, and can lead to new and unforeseen exegetical results.

2. Structuralism offers a new role and status to the biblical critic by making him in a sense a participant in the text which he reads. The critic thus does not decipher the meaning of a biblical text, but actively formulates in his own mind the structures underlying the meaning. Hence the task of the critic is to reconstruct the very being of biblical literature, which lies, or so structuralists in general maintain, in its system of signs. As Barthes has observed, the critic *creates* the finished work by his reading of it, and does not remain simply the inert consumer of a ready-made product. Doubrovsky has commented in this regard: "Racine exists in the readings of Racine, and apart from the readings there is no Racine."[10] In the same context, scripture exists in the readings of scripture; the critic creates it by his reading of it. However, the special danger to which any reader of scripture is subject

is eisegesis: critics and readers of the Bible always have to be on the alert against reading unjustifiable meanings into the text, eisegetically, while at the same time recreating the finished work.

While holding the view that structuralist methodologies can aid exegesis and hermeneutics in these ways, I would emphasize that their advantages should not be exaggerated. The analyst using structural methods should always be aware of their limitations, several of which have been mentioned in earlier chapters. Five in particular bear reiteration:

1. As a general rule, structuralist methodologies do not take into account the inspired nature of the biblical text. The fact that the biblical authors wrote as they did was not, I maintain, primarily the result of grammatical forces, as is advocated by Güttgemanns. On the contrary, the biblical authors sometimes knowingly and at other times unknowingly were recipients of divine guidance: even though few scholars today would argue for verbal inspiration, it is certainly reasonable to see some element of Godly assistance both in the writing of the sacred text and in the canonization process which determined the limits of textual inspiration.

2. In common with E.D. Hirsch, I maintain that a text cannot validly be *interpreted* from a perspective different from the original author's.[11] Clearly, no biblical author had a structuralist perspective. I doubt very much if structuralist interpretation could be included within any theory of the *sensus plenior* of the text. It follows, therefore, that structuralist methods should be used as a general rule for analysis rather than for interpretation.

3. The structuralist is not principally concerned with meaning, though clearly the meaning of the text which he is analyzing must be of some importance to him. Interpretations of meaning in scripture will always fall to scholars of Hebrew, Aramaic and Greek using exegetical methods, rather than to structuralist critics.

4. It is a generally held structuralist position that the medium of

of a text is its message; in other words, literary works are self-reflective and ultimately *about* language. This viewpoint justifies the post-romantic notion that form and content are one, a concept that is well exemplified in Todorov's statement that the ultimate subject of *The Thousand and One Nights* is the act of story telling itself. However, such an attitude, I submit, is more appropriate to pure fiction than to biblical literature, in which the kerygma, not the medium, is the principal message. Indeed, form criticism has demonstrated how much of the New Testament text has been shaped by the kerygma: its influence on the text was formative in a sense that purely linguistic forces were not.

5. Structuralist methodologies are all relatively new and still for all practical purposes experimental.

At present there is no general consensus of opinion on the value of structuralist procedures. Some observers view structuralism as a passing fad, others see it as providing an outlook of permanent value.[12] Its practitioners have no doubt made exaggerated claims for its usefulness when a more modest attitude would have been appropriate. Pleas to the effect that structuralism will in the future reveal the basic structures of human thought need to be revised: there is today little tangible evidence to support grandiose representations of this kind. But structural methodologies can provide a degree of semiotic assistance to the biblical scholar, provided that he is willing to concede a more important status to the inspired character of the sacred text than to the particular structuralist procedure which be is utilizing.

Since this book is devoted to structuralist interpretations of sacred scripture, it would be inappropriate to discuss post-structuralist methods. Critics of structuralism have emphasized its shortcomings and done much to convert wavering structuralists into curious or even convinced deconstructionists. The difference between structuralists and their successors has been well summarized by Jonathan Culler: "Structuralists are convinced that systematic knowledge is possible: post-structuralists claim to know only the impossibility of this knowledge."[13] But for the

scholar concerned with the effect of deconstructionism on scriptural hermeneutics there is a collection of essays in *Semeia*, Vol. 23, 1982 entitled "Derrida and Biblical Studies," which includes two contributions by Derrida himself. His repudiation of the Christian *logos* and his enigmatic proposition that writing is prior to speech have done little to endear him to biblical theologians or exegetes in general. The validity of Derrida's principle *"Il n'y a pas de hors-texte"* is questionable, especially when the text is seen as having no stable origin or identity, and each act of reading "the text" is conceived of primarily as a preface to the next.

Norris's definition of deconstruction as "the active antithesis of everything that criticism ought to be if one accepts its traditional values and concepts" is surely justifiable.[14] However, Derrida's work has had some benign influences on individual structuralists. Thus J.D. Crossan, in his structuralist analysis of John 6, has been patently influenced by several aspects of Derrida's early thinking.[15] Though structuralism and deconstructionism are methodologically separable, the Proteus-like nature of structuralism has in recent years acquired a certain deconstructionist character in the hands of some of its practitioners. It remains to be seen how far deconstructionist thinking will modify the application of historically structuralist principles to the text of sacred scripture.

Notes

1.   The first English translation had appeared in 1958.
2.   John Hick (ed.), *The Myth of God Incarnate* (Philadelphia: Westminster Press, 1977). Wiles's essay, "Myth in Theology," is to be found on pp. 148-166.
3.   Some relevant remarks by Peter Hodgson on Strauss's mythical point of view are contained in the "Introduction" to his edition of George Eliot's translation of *Das Leben Jesu, kritisch bearbeitet,* published by Fortress Press in 1972. For

my review of Hodgson's edition see *The Catholic Biblical Quarterly*, Vol. 36 (January 1974), pp. 144 f.

4. John Hick (ed.), *op. cit.*, p. 161.

5. See Emmon Bach, "Structural Linguistics and the Philosophy of Science," *Diogenes*, Vol. 51 (1965), pp. 111-128, and Jean Piaget, *Structuralism* (New York: Basic Books, 1968).

6. See Raymond Boudon, *A Quoi sert la Notion de Structure?* (Paris: Editions Gallimard, 1968), and Karl Popper, *The Logic of Scientific Discovery* (New York: Harper & Row, 1968).

7. For example, Pierre Guiraud, *Problèmes et Méthodes de la Statistique Linguistique* (Dordrecht: Reidel, 1960), and A. Ellegård, *A Statistical Method for Determining Authorship* (Gothenburg Studies in English, 1962). I have discussed the use of stylostatistics in relation to the biblical text in my article, "Rhetorical Criticism and *Formgeschichte*: Some Methodological Considerations," *Journal of Biblical Literature*, Vol. 89 (1970), pp. 418-426. Some of the rationale in this article is repeated here.

8. I assume as a given that the Bible has a kerygmatic content, though the term *kerygma*, especially as used in the works of Bultmann, is somewhat ambiguous.

9. Hans Gadamer, *Truth and Method* (New York: Seabury Press, 1975), especially pp. 366-397. See also the excellent short treatment of Gadamer's fundamental position in Richard E. Palmer, *Hermeneutics* (Evanston: Northwestern University Press, 1969), pp. 162-217.

10. Serge Doubrovsky, *The New Criticism in France* (Chicago: University of Chicago Press, 1973), p. 7. On this matter Barthes and Doubrovsky hold very similar positions. Some theologians maintain a comparable position on the subject of *kerygma*.

11. See E.D. Hirsch, *The Aims of Interpretation* (Chicago: University of Chicago Press, 1976), especially pp. 36-49.

12. On structuralism as a fad see George Watson, "Chomsky: What Has It to do with Literature," *The Times Literary Supplement*, (February 14, 1975), pp. 164-165. Watson is of the opinion that structuralism since the 1960s has "shifted forlornly into that rag-and-bone heap of discredited notions known as Modern Critical Thought, where its assumptions still form the decaying foundations of literary structuralism and its numerous intellectual outhouses." He further maintains that Chomsky thinks structuralism to be "bunkum." See also Graham Hough, "The Importation of Roland Barthes," *The Times Literary Supplement* (December 9, 1977), pp. 1443, where Hough comments that Paris fashions change very quickly, "including the one to which Barthes has mostly adhered" [i.e., structuralism].

13. Jonathan Culler, *On Deconstruction: Theory and Criticism after Structuralism* (Ithaca: Cornell University Press, 1982). For an excellent review of this work by John R. Searle see "The Word Turned Upside Down" in *The New York Review of Books* (October 27, 1983), pp. 74-79.

14. Christopher Norris, *Deconstruction: Theory and Practice* (London: Methuen, 1982), p. xii. For more evidence to support Norris's position see the exhaustive critique of Derrida's theory of signs and his deconstructivism in T.K. Seung, *Structuralism and Hermeneutics* (New York: Columbia University Press, 1982), esp. chapters 6, 7 and 10.

15. J.D. Crossan, "It is written: A Structuralist Analysis of John 6," *Semeia*, Vol. 26, 1983, pp. 3-21.

Structural Analysis

The methodology employed in the two structural analyses which follow is, like that of Dan Via, moderately eclectic, though the influence of Barthes and Greimas will be readily apparent. My indebtedness to Saussure and Lévi-Strauss is, of couse, implicit in the nature of this type of textual interpretation. As a matter of convenience, I include the full text of each passage to be analyzed. The version used is the New English Bible.

I

The Ordeal of Isaac: Genesis 22:1-19

The time came when God put Abraham to the test. 'Abraham,' he called, and Abraham replied, 'Here I am.' God said, 'Take your son Isaac, your only son, whom you love, and go the land of Moriah. There you shall offer him as a sacrifice on one of the hills which I will show you.' So Abraham rose early in the morning and saddled his ass, and he took with him two of his men and his son, Isaac; and he split the firewood for the sacrifice, and set out for the place of which God had spoken. On the third day Abraham looked up and saw the place in the distance. He said to his men, 'Stay here with the ass while I and the boy go over there; and when we have worshipped we will come back to you.' So Abraham took the wood for the sacrifice and laid it on his son Isaac's shoulder; he himself carried the fire and the knife, and the two of them went on together. Isaac said to Abraham, 'Father,' and he answered, 'What is it, my son?' Isaac said, 'Here are the fire and the wood, but where is the young beast for the sacrifice?' Abraham answered, 'God will provide himself with a young beast for the sacrifice, my son.' And the two of them went on together and came to the place of which God had spoken. There Abraham built an altar and arranged the wood. He bound his son Isaac and laid him on the altar on top of the wood. Then he stretched out his hand and took the knife to kill his son; but the angel of the LORD called to him from heaven, 'Abraham, Abraham.' He answered, 'Here I am.' The angel of the Lord said, 'Do not raise your hand against the boy; do not touch

him. Now I know that you are a God-fearing man. You have not withheld from me your son, your only son.' Abraham looked up, and there he saw a ram caught by its horns in a thicket. So he went and took the ram and offered it as a sacrifice instead of his son. Abraham named that place Jehovahjireh; and to this day the saying is: 'In the mountain of the LORD it was provided.' Then the angel of the LORD called from heaven a second time to Abraham, 'This is the word of the LORD: By my own self I swear; inasmuch as you have done this and have not withheld your son, your only son, I will bless you abundantly and greatly multiply your descendants until they are as numerous as the stars in the sky and the grains of sand on the sea-shore. Your descendants shall possess the cities of their enemies. All nations on earth shall pray to be blessed as your descendants are blessed, and this because you have obeyed me.' Abraham went back to his men, and together they returned to Beersheba; and there Abraham remained.

Initial comments

This story should be seen in the context of Genesis as a whole, and in particular in relation to the promissory sequences of that book, even though this context cannot here be analyzed in detail. A son was promised implicitly to Abraham in Genesis 12:1-3, and explicitly in Genesis 15, especially in verses 4, 5. Now that the promise has been fulfilled, the son is to be sacrificed, though the sacrifice sequence is concluded before the end of the story. This narrative-unit is not indubitably a myth, and cannot therefore be treated as a mythological text. Furthermore, there is a definite moral argument implicitly underlying the story; essentially it is that faith in God will be rewarded. Some commentators have seen a secondary moral argument inherent in the text, to the effect that the sacrifice of an animal may legitimize the redemption of child sacrifice. But a mythological text, at least as understood by Lévi-Strauss, does not have a conscious, logical argument. Its structures are primarily deep structures, and there is only very limited interference from other structures. I view the story of the ordeal of Isaac simply as a narrative-unit within the larger context of the Genesis narrative. The "plot" is uncomplicated and there is no sub-plot. The fact that this story does not appear to be a

clear case of myth is not a denial of its mythic structure. As has already been averred in Chapter II, mythic structures can be discerned even in patently non-mythological texts.

Lexie 1: The time came when God put Abraham to the test. 'Abraham,' he called, and Abraham replied, 'Here I am.' God said, 'Take your son Isaac, your only son, whom you love, and go the land of Moriah. There you shall offer him as a sacrifice on one of the hills which I shall show you.'

This lexie begins with a specific summons to Abraham by name, followed by a mandate to sacrifice his son Isaac. The comment "God put Abraham to the test" is unusual: the implication is that his faith is being tested. To appreciate the semiotic significance of the sacrificial mandate, one should see it in relation to the denotative content of the promise made in Genesis 12:1-3. The sacrificial mandate and the previous promise might seem to stand in striking contradiction to each other. But in fact the mandate is not in contradiction to the particular form of the promise, which actually provided nothing material. Furthermore, it demanded faith as an implied condition of its validity. If Abraham had not had faith in God's word, the promise might never have been fulfilled. This lexie indicates that Abraham's faith is not to be tested in terms of God's mandate. In the terminology of Greimas, the three actants are God, who constitutes the subject; Abraham, who constitutes the object; and Isaac, who is the helper, since he is initially indicated as the individual who will enable Abraham to fulfill his obligation in the context of his convenantal (or in structuralist terms, contractual) relationship with God. In the first sentence the effect is heightened by the use of the definite article with *Elohim*. Structural parallelism is later manifested in the use of the triple imperative (take, go, offer). Among the syntactic features of this lexie is the affective clause relating to Isaac, "whom you love." Affective terminology is used sparingly in this story. The use of the particle of entreaty *na'* in the initial imperative is also syntactically significant: very rarely in biblical literature does *na'* appear in a divine command. It underlies the

monstrosity of the command, and the fact that God is well aware of its true nature.

Lexie 2:   So Abraham rose early in the morning and saddled his ass, and he took with him two of his men and his son, Isaac; and he split the firewood for the sacrifice, and set out for the place of which God had spoken.

Abraham's obedience to his contractual obligations is exemplary: he clearly evinces the faith which is implicitly necessary in Lexie 1. There is no structurally parallel reply by Abraham to God's command in Lexie 1; Abraham does the will of God without murmur. Sarah (who is not mentioned in this narrative unit, but is an actant in Chapter 21) remains behind at Beersheba, blissfully ignorant of her husband's dreadful mission.

Lexie 3:   On the third day Abraham looked up and saw the place in the distance. He said to his men, 'Stay here with the ass while I and the boy go over there; and when we have worshipped we will come back to you.'

This lexie constitutes a performancial syntagm in the Abraham sequence only. The brief narrative of the two men temporarily concludes here; at the end of the story they return to Beersheba with Abraham. Interestingly, no indication is later given to Isaac's departure from the mountain: when he next appears in the Genesis narrative (24:62) he is at Beer-lahai-roi.

Lexie 4:   So Abraham took the wood for the sacrifice and laid it on his son Isaac's shoulder; he himself carried the fire and the knife and the two of them went on together.

In this lexie the Abraham and Isaac sequences run parallel and approach the acme of the story together. The formulaic expression, "the two of them went on together" covers a uniquely poignant and eloquent silence.

Lexie 5:   Isaac said to Abraham, 'Father,' and he answered, 'What is it, my son?' Isaac said, 'Here are the fire and the wood, but

where is the young beast for the sacrifice?' Abraham answered, 'God will provide himself with a young beast for a sacrifice, my son.' And the two of them went on together and came to the place of which God had spoken.

The intertwining of the Abraham and Isaac sequences at this point is achieved with extraordinary tenderness. In terms of the textual surface, the short, staccato sentences in this and the following lexie produce a remarkable somnambulistic effect.

Lexie 6:   There Abraham built an altar and arranged the wood. He bound his son Isaac and laid him on the altar on top of the wood. Then he stretched out his hand and took the knife to kill his son; but the angel of the Lord called to him from heaven, 'Abraham, Abraham,' He answered, 'Here I am.'

The most significant characteristic of this lexie is the absence of confrontation or even opposition on the part of Isaac. The implication of this absence would seem to be that Isaac regarded himself as having the same contractual relationship as his father to Yahweh. Faith in God presumes obedience to His will. The angel is a literary device; in everything that he declaims the voice of God is evident.

Lexie 7:   The angel of the Lord said, 'Do not raise your hand against the boy; do not touch him. Now I know that you are a God-fearing man. You have not withheld from me your son, your only son.'

The qualifying test of Abraham's faith is now successfully concluded. It has resulted in a restoration of the original situation or a *regressus ad initium*. The movement of the story is thus circular in terms of its mythical structure. The details that follow, including the subsequent promise of the angel, are in a sense structural additions to the plot. The term "God-fearing man" is formulaic: it occurs with some frequency in the works of the prophets. It implies absolute dedication rather than "fear" in the usual sence.

Lexie 8:   Abraham looked up, and there he saw a ram caught by its horns in a thicket. So he went and took the ram and offered it as a sacrifice instead

of his son. Abraham named that place Jehovah-jireh; and to this day the saying is: 'In the mountain of the Lord it was provided.'

In the opinion of Von Rad, the narrative once concluded at this point, and the subsequent second speech of the angel constitutes an addition to the ancient cultic legend.[1] The sacrifice of the ram by Abraham is quite voluntary: according to Leviticus 1:10-13 the ram was a usual victim for holocausts. This sacrifice might be interpreted as a spontaneous exhibition of heartfelt gratitude to God that Isaac's life had been spared. The emotional overtones, though subdued and refined, are rich: even in the quasi-philological notice about the name of the place, Abraham's intention is clearly one of thanksgiving. The translation of Jehovah-jireh in the NEB should be compared to that given by Speiser in his edition of Genesis: by allowing for the possible repointing of *yhwh yr'h* he arrives at the meaning, "On Yahweh's mountain there is vision." Neither translation has won universal acceptance, but this matter is a problem of vocalization rather than structure.[2]

Lexie 9:   Then the angel of the Lord called from heaven a second time to Abraham, 'This is the word of the Lord: By my own self I swear: inasmuch as you have done this and have not withheld your son, your only son, I will bless you abundantly and greatly multiply your descendants until they are as numerous as the stars in the sky and the grains of sand on the sea-shore. Your descendants shall possess the cities of their enemies. All nations on earth shall pray to be blessed as your descendants are blessed, and this because you have obeyed me.'

The primary concern in this lexie is to link the main narrative of this story with the motif of promise, the motif which thematically unites all the Abrahamic narratives. Stylistically this lexie is much removed from the restrained representation in the main narrative: God Himself is made to use the official formula of the later prophets. "This is the word of the Lord," and is also made to swear "By my own self," a usage that has no parallel in any comparable context. The promise that Abraham's descendants would possess the cities of their enemies is one which is contextually foreign to

the basis of the other promises. The use of Hithpael (hitbārăkû) instead of the Niphal in the last sentence of this lexie conveys a reflexive connotation; the modality of the Hebrew text is thus closer to "in your descendants all nations on earth shall bless themselves." Hence the meaning-value of this sentence is that Abraham's descendants will be a formula of blessing for others. The angel sequence ends here: no indication is given as to whether or not it was a success or a failure (in the sense of its prophetical content being fulfilled or unfulfilled). The angel's proposed program therefore remains potential, unactualized, and unsemant- ized, but it nevertheless constitutes an essential part of the con- tractual relationship between God and Abraham, and of the contractual syntagm in which it occurs.

Lexie 10: Abraham went back to his men, and together they returned to Beersheba; and there Abraham remained.

This lexie concludes the Abrahamic sequence and also the narrative of the two men, which was temporarily dropped in lexie 3. No mention is made of the return of Isaac: his sequence is therefore left incomplete.

II

The Prodigal Son: Luke 15:11-32

There was once a man who had two sons; and the younger said to his father, 'Father, give me my share of the property.' So he divided his estate between them. A few days later the younger son turned the whole of his share into cash and left home for a distant country, where he squandered it in reckless living. He had spent it all, when a severe famine fell upon that country and he began to feel the pinch. So he went and attached himself to one of the local landowners, who sent him on to his farm to mind the pigs. He would have been glad to fill his belly with the pods that the pigs were eating; and no one gave him anything. Then he came to his senses and said, 'How many of my father's paid servants have more food than they can eat, and here am I, starving to death! I will set off and go to my father, and say to him, 'Father,

I have sinned, against God and against you; I am no longer fit to be called your son; treat me as one of your paid servants.' So he set out for his father's house. But while he was still a long way off his father saw him and his heart went out to him. He ran to meet him, flung his arms round him, and kissed him. The son said, 'Father, I have sinned, against God and against you; I am no longer fit to be called your son.' But the father said to his servants, 'Quick! fetch a robe, my best one, and put it on him; put a ring on his finger and shoes on his feet. Bring the fatted calf and kill it, and let us have a feast to celebrate the day. For this son of mine was dead and has come back to life; he was lost and is found.' And the festivities began.

Now the elder son was out on the farm; and on his way back as he approached the house he heard music and dancing. He called one of the servants and asked what it meant. The servant told him, 'Your brother has come home, and your father has killed the fatted calf because he has him back safe and sound.' But he was angry and refused to go in. His father came out and pleaded with him; but he retorted,'You know how I have slaved for you all these years; I never once disobeyed your orders; and you never gave me so much as a kid, for a feast with my friends. But now that this son of yours turns up, after running through your money with his women, you kill the fatted calf for him.' 'My boy,' said the father, 'you are always with me, and everything I have is yours. How could we help celebrating this happy day? Your brother here was dead and has come back to life, was lost and is found.'

Initial comments

The Gospel of Luke as a whole is a complex narrative in which are embedded multiple sub-narratives. A parable is one of those sub-narratives which is in itself a complete narrative. As sub-narrative it contributes to the general meaning of the entire gospel, and conversely, the fact that it is embedded in the gospel contributes to the meaning of the parable. However, it would be impossible in this analysis to deal in detail with the relationship between this sub-narrative and the rest of the Lucan gospel. Such a study would demand the structural analysis of the entire Lucan gospel narrative. The relationship between parable and gospel is therefore dealt with only to the extent to which it illuminates the matters discussed in the lexie commentaries. This necessary limitation provides yet another corroboration of the well known structuralist dictum that no structural analysis is ever complete.

The narrative structure of this parable contains two initial correlated sequences, one in which the father divides the property, and one in which the younger son loses his share. In the initial correlated sub-sequence the younger son squanders his property, thus destroying his well-being and threatening his father's contract. In two topical sequences the younger son seeks to establish his well-being, first in spending money, and then by attaching himself to one of the local landowners. Both of these sequences are aborted. In a subsequent correlated sequence the father re-establishes the younger son's well-being and his contractual relationship to him. In the second part of the parable the sequences relating to the elder son are presented in deliberate contrast to the story of the younger son. It should be remarked that the majority of sequences are only partially actualized: because a narrative sequence is part of the deep structure, the mention of a few of its features should generally be sufficient to evoke a whole sequence.

Lexie 1:   There was once a man who had two sons.

This lexie introduces three actants: the father, who constitutes the subject, and the two sons, who together constitute the object. They are presented *in vacuo*. No information is given as to who they were, in which country or place they were living, or their previous history. The *Sitz im Leben* is not entirely clear either. We do not know where these words were delivered, though Luke 15:1-2 indicate that they were addressed to a crowd of persons including tax-gatherers, Pharisees, and doctors of the law. Louise Schottroff has argued that there was no authentic *Sitz im Leben*, and that the entire parable is the creation of Luke himself.[3] However, Sanders has provided sufficient evidence to demonstrate the semitic background of the parable; Schottroff's case for original Lucan composition may therefore be dismissed.[4]

Lexie 2:   And the younger said to his father, 'Father, give me my share of the property.'

This lexie introduces the first sequence which manifests a contractual relationship between the younger son (here the addresser) and the father (here the subject who communicates the object, i.e., the share of the property, to the recipient, i.e., the younger son).

Lexie 3:   So he divided his estate between them.

The father agrees to his younger son's request; in other words, the father's mandate has been successfully carried out in the initial correlated sequence. Four actants are semantized in this syntagm.

Subject   : Father
Object   : Estate
Addressees   : The younger and elder sons.

Lexie 4:   A few days later the younger son turned the whole of his share into cash and left home for a distant country.

At the level of manifestation this utterance is recognized by the function of departure and arrival: departure from his father's home, arrival in a distant country. Because this is a disjunctional syntagm, the subject, the younger son, has accepted a contract which is not specified at the level of manifestation. The implied contract more probably is that he will use the cash for his well-being. This disjunctional syntagm is part of the initial correlated sequence of the subsequence of the younger's son's narrative.

Lexie 5:   . . . where he squandered it in reckless living. He had spent it all, when a severe famine fell upon that country and he began to feel the pinch.

This lexie constitutes a performancial syntagm. The function of submission is manifested so that the subsequence of the younger son is now concluded. The purpose of the topical sequences that follow will be to establish the original contract, the son's well-being. Two opponents are semantized in this syntagm. On the one

hand the younger son is his own opponent for he squanders his money in loose living, and the other opponent is the famine. Hence the younger son passes from well-being to lack of well-being.

Lexie 6:   So he went and attached himself to one of the local landowners.

This lexie constitutes a disjunctional syntagm, which concludes the initial correlated subsequence of the younger son. Since the younger son is his own opponent, he must overcome himself in order to complete his part of the contractual relationship with his father.

Lexie 7:   . . . who sent him on to his farm to mind the pigs.

The contract between the younger son and the local landowner is now semantized. The duty of the son is "to mind the pigs." There are at this point in the parable two actantial models, since the stories of the younger son and the landowner have intercepted. At the level of manifestation this lexie represents the semantization of the narrative of the landowner, but in the narrative structure it is a subsequence of the narrative of the younger son. In the younger son's narrative this lexie is a disjunctional syntagm, since his going on to the farm denotes his acceptance of the contract offered by the landowner.

Lexie 8:   He would have been glad to fill his belly with the pods that the pigs were eating; and no one gave him anything.

In this lexie the syntagm returns to the story of the younger son from that of the landowner. The functions are confrontation and domination. A new program is proposed which remains potential, as the modalities "would have been glad" and "no one gave him anything" clearly indicate. Hence this particular sequence is not developed further.

Lexie 9:   Then he came to his senses and said "How many of my father's paid servants have more food than they can eat, and here I am, starving to

death! I will set off and go to my father, and say to him, 'Father, I have
sinned against God and against you; I am no longer fit to be called your son;
treat me as one of your paid servants.'

This lexie constitutes the first utterance of a contractual syntagm,
in which the younger son proposes a contract to his father, the
purpose of which is the establishment of the son's original contract, i.e., his well-being. The future tense modality makes this
lexie a proposed program rather than an actual performance. The
sequence stops at "treat me as one of your paid servants": This
part of the proposed message is never actually delivered to the
father.

Lexie 10:   So he set out for his father's house.

This lexie constitutes a disjunctional syntagm which reinforces
the substance of lexie 9. The younger son, who has been one of
his own opponents, must propose a new contract to his father if
he is to accomplish his original contract. We should therefore
expect to encounter shortly a performancial syntagm in which
the younger son approaches his father with a view to his accepting
this new contract. The first part of this performancial syntagm
will occur in lexie 12.

Lexie 11:   But while he was still a long way off his father saw him, and his
heart went out to him. He ran to meet him.

This lexie constitutes a return to the father's story, which was
abandoned after lexie 3. The function of departure, "ran," marks
this lexie as a disjunctional syntagm. The modality of the sequence
is expressed in the phrase "while he was still a long way off,"
which emphasizes the eagerness of the father to carry out this
program. The original program of the son is, of course, nullified
by the father's program.

Lexie 12:   . . . flung his arms round him, and kissed him.

This lexie constitutes the first part of the performancial syntagm, in which the father as subject dominates the younger son. The syntagm will be completed in lexie 14.

Lexie 13:   The son said, 'Father, I have sinned, against God and against you; I am no longer fit to be called your son.'

This lexie entails the function of submissive confrontation. The new contract which is implied is not here fully semantized. This lexie, like lexie 12, is part of a performancial syntagm, but only in the younger son's sequence.

Lexie 14:   But the father said to his servants, 'Quick! fetch a robe, my best one, and put it on him; put a ring on his finger and shoes on his feet. Bring the fatted calf and kill it, and let us have a feast to celebrate the day.'

In this lexie the father, who dominated his younger son in lexie 12, now completes the performancial syntagm started in that lexie. The father's contract is not fully semantized until lexie 15. There is no explicit indication that the father's mandates in this lexie are actually performed, but the connotative implication is that they are.

Lexie 15:   'For this son of mine was dead and has come back to life; he was lost and is found.' And the festivities began.

The stories of both the father and the younger son are here summarized. "Was dead and has come back to life" summarizes the story of the younger son; "was lost and is found" summarizes the story of the father. The contract of the father is here semantized by the repossession of his younger son. Now the elder son has to be dealt with.

Lexie 16:   Now the elder son was out on the farm.

This lexie introduces the story of the elder son, whose existence was implied in lexie 1. But more than simply introducing the

elder son, it locates his narrative to this point as being intertwined with that of the father. This fact is shown by the information that he was on the farm, i.e., he has remained within the father's network. Likewise, since he was on the farm, he was not part of the reception of the younger son and therefore has not ratified the father's contract. The qualification sets up the situation in which the elder son must either continue his story with that of the father or withdraw from the father's structural network.

Lexie 17:   And on his way back, as he approached the house, he heard music and dancing.

This utterance is characterized at the level of manifestation by the function of departure and arrival, and therefore appears to be a disjunctional syntagm which implies the acceptance of a contract. But it should be noted that at the level of manifestation the function of arrival is not completed: ". . . as he approached." Therefore this utterance indicates that the sequence will deal with the acceptance or rejection of a contract. If the elder son completes the function of arrival, then the contract is accepted; if he does not, then the contract is rejected. The elder son has a contract to accept a contract. This disjunctional syntagm points to the problematic of this narrative as revolving around the completion or abortion of the implied contractual arrangements.

Lexie 18:   He called one of the servants and asked what it meant. The servant told him, 'Your brother has come home, and your father has killed the fatted calf because he has him back safe and sound.'

The contract of the elder brother is the acceptance of a contract. In this lexie the contract to be accepted is revealed, the father's acceptance of the younger son. This syntagm involves the function of confrontation; the elder brother is confronted with the contract which he has a contract to accept.

Lexie 19:   "But he was angry and refused to go in.

In this lexie the elder brother rejects his father's contract, and his narrative now comes to an end.

Lexie 20:   His father came out and pleaded with him.

In this lexie there are two syntagms, a disjunctional and a performancial. By coming out, the father has accepted a contract to entreat the elder son to come in, i.e., to accept the father's contract with the younger son. By entreating, the father engages in the function of confrontation.

Lexie 21:   . . . but he retorted, 'You know how I have slaved for you all these years; I never once disobeyed your orders; and you never once gave me so much as a kid, for a feast with my friends. But now that this son of yours turns up, after running through your money with his women, you kill the fatted calf for him.'

The sequence to this point has concerned the elder son's acceptance or rejection of the contract his father made with the younger son. The subject has clearly remained the elder son. But implied within this sequence is the possibility that the elder son represents an opponent to the father's original contract, namely the having of two sons. In this lexie that original contract comes directly to the surface. The elder son by addressing the father designates him subject and confronts him about the terms of the original contract. This fact can be seen at the level of manifestation by the clear division between the elder and younger brother, "this son of yours," and the accusation that he, the elder brother, has not been treated as a son. The elder son is now clearly an opponent to the original contract of the parable: "A certain man had two sons." This lexie commences the final correlated sequence. The expression "you kill the fatted calf" should not be taken literally: in lexie 14 the servants were ordered to do the killing.

Lexie 22:   'My boy,' said the father, 'you are always with me, and everything I have is yours. How could we help celebrating this happy day? Your brother here was dead and has come back to life, was lost and is found.'

In this final lexie the father refuses to allow the elder son to dominate him or to reject him. The parable thus ends, as it began, with the father living with his two sons. "You are always with me" summarizes and concludes the elder son's sequence.

Notes

1.   Gerhard von Rad, *Genesis* (Philadelphia: Westminster Press, 1972), p. 242.
2.   See E.A. Speiser, *Genesis* (New York: Doubleday, 1964), pp. 163 f. Other translations include "In the mount of the Lord it shall be seen" (KJV); "On the mountain the Lord will see" (NAB); "On the mountain Yahweh provides" (Jerusalem Bible). It is possible that Jehovah-jireh was not a place name at all, but only a pun which at one time explained a place name. It is not semantically precise: there is no indication as to what was provided or seen on the mountain.
3.   Louise Schottroff, "Das Gleichnis vom verlorenen Sohn," *Zeitschrift für Theologie und Kirche*, Vol. 68 (1971), pp. 27-52.
4.   J. Sanders, "Tradition and Redaction in Luke XV:11-32," *New Testament Studies,* Vol. 15 (1969), pp. 433-438.

Select Bibliography

This bibliography is intended to provide a list of the principal materials relevant to biblical structuralism. It contains works of somewhat unequal quality, though every item here included is germane in some respect or other to the subject of structuralism and the biblical text. It is divided into two sections, the first providing a list of the principal books and articles which are relevant to the topic, and the second a list of journal issues devoted entirely or largely to structural analysis.

I: Principal Books and Articles

Amphoux, C.B. (1973), "Etudes structurales: Langue de l'Epitre de Jacques." *Revue d'Histoire et de Philosophie Religieuses*, 53: 7-45.

ApRoberts, Ruth (1977), "Old Testament Poetry: The Translatable Structure." *Publications of the Modern Language Association of America*, 92: 987-1003.

Auzias, J.M. (1967), *Clefs pour le structuralisme*. Paris: Seghers.

Bachelard, G. (1964), *The Psychoanalysis of Fire*. Translated by Alan C. Ross. London: Routledge.

Balakian, A.E. (1967), *The Symbolist Movement: A Critical Approach*. New York: Random House.

Bann, S. and Bowlt, J.E. (1973), *Russian Formalism*. New York: Barnes & Noble.

Bar, Eugen. (1971), "The Language of the Unconscious According to Jacques Lacan." *Semiotica*, 3: 241-68.

Barr, J. (1973), *The Bible in the Modern World*. New York: Harper & Row.

– (1969), *Biblical Words for Time*. Naperville, Ill.: Allenson.

– (1984), *Holy Scripture: Canon, Authority, Criticism*. Oxford: Clarendon Press.

– (1961), *The Semantics of Biblical Language*. London: Oxford University Press.

– (1972), "Semantics and Biblical Theology: A Contribution to the Discussion." In *Supplements to Vetus Testamentum*, 22, pp. 11-19. Leiden: E.J. Brill.

Barthel, P. (1963), *Interprétation du langage mythique et théologie biblique. Étude de quelques étapes de l'évolution du problème de l'interprétation des représentations d'origine et de structure mythiques de la foi chrétienne*. Leiden: E.J. Brill.

Barthes, R. (1970), "L'Analyse structurale du récit. A Propos d'Actes X-XI." *Recherches de Science Religieuse* 58: 17-37 (reprinted in Léon-Dufour, *Exégèse et Herméneutique*).

– (1972), *Critical Essays*. Translated by Richard Howard. Evanston: Northwestern University Press.

– (1963), "Criticism as Language." *The Times Literary Supplement* 3213: 739-40.

Barthes, R. (1966), *Critique et vérité*. Paris: Editions du Seuil.
— (1969), *Elements of Semiology*. Translated by Annette Lavers and Colin Smith. London: Johathan Cape.
— (1970), *l'Empire des signes*. Geneva: Albert Skira.
— (1977), *Image, Music, Text*. Translated by Stephen Heath. New York: Hill & Wang.
— (1966), "Introduction à l'analyse structurale des récits." *Communication* 8: 1-27.
— (1971), "La lutte avec l'ange: Analyse textuelle de Genèse 32, 23-33." *Analyse structurale et exégèse biblique*. Neuchâtel: Delachaux et Niestlé.
— (1972), *Mythologies*. Translated by Annette Lavers. New York: Hill & Wang.
— (1973), *Le plaisir du texte*. Paris: Editions du Seuil.
— (1967), "Science versus Literature." *The Times Literary Supplement* 3422: 897-98.
— (1962), "Sociologie et socio-logique: A propos de deux ouvrages recentes de Claude Lévi-Strauss." *Information sur les Sciences Sociales* 1: 114-22.
— (1967), "The Structuralist Activity." *Partisan Review* 34: 83-88.
— (1967), *Système de la mode*. Paris: Editions du Seuil.
— (1970), *S/Z*. Paris: Editions du Seuil.
— (1970), *Writing Degree Zero*. Translated by Annette Lavers and Colin Smith. New York: Hill & Wang, 1968; Boston: Beacon Press.
Bastide, Roger (1962), ed. *Sens et usages du terme "structure."* The Hague: Mouton.
Beauchamp, Paul (1972), "l'Analyse structurale et l'exégèse biblique." *Supplements to Vetus Testamentum*, 22, pp. 113-28.
— (1969), *Création et Séparation*. Paris: Delachaux et Niestlé.
— (1971), *Leçons sur l'exégèse*. Lyon: Polycopié.
— (1970), "Proposition sur l'alliance de l'AT comme structure centrale." *Recherches de Science Religieuse* 58: 161-93.
Becker, Ernest (1968), *The Structure of Evil: An Essay on the Unification of the Science of Man*. New York: George Braziller.
Bersani, Leo (1967), "From Bachelard to Barthes." *Partisan Review* 34: 215-32.
Blancy, A. (1973), "Structuralisme et herméneutique." *Études Théologiques et Religieuses* 48: 49-60.
Bogaert, M. (1968), "Structure et message de la Première Epître de saint Jean." *Bible et Vie Chrétienne* 83: 33-45.
Bohannan, Paul (1960), "Conscience, Collective and Culture." In Emile Durkheim *et al. Essays on Sociology and Philosophy*, pp. 77-96. Edited by K.H. Wolff. New York: Harper Torchbooks.
Boon, James A. (1972), *From Symbolism to Structuralism: Lévi-Strauss in a Literary Tradition*. New York: Harper Torchbooks.
— (1970), "Lévi-Strauss and Narrative." *Man* 5: 702-03.
Boudon, Raymond (1971), *The Uses of Structuralism*. Translated by Michalina Baughan. London: Heinemann Educational Books.
Bourdieu, P. (1968), "Structuralism and Theory of Social Knowledge." *Social Research* 35: 681-706.
— and Passeron, J.C. (1967), "Sociology and Philosophy in France since 1945: Death and Resurrection of a Philosophy without Subject." *Social Research* 34: 162-212.
Bouttier, Michel (1973), "A nos lecteurs et amis." *Études Théologiques et Religieuses* 48: 1-2.
Bovon, François (1971), ed. *Analyse structurale et exégèse biblique*. Neuchâtel: Delachaux & Niestlé.
— (1971), "Strukturalismus und biblische Exégèse." *Wissenschaft und Praxis in Kirche und Gesellschaft* 60: 16-26.
Breymayer, R. (1972), "Zur Pragmatik des Bildes. Semiotische Beobachtungen zum Streitgespräch Mk 12, 13-17 ('Der Zinsgroschen') unter Berücksichtigung der Spieltheorie." *Linguistica Biblica* 13-14: 19-51.

Buchler, I.E. and Selby, H.A. (1968), *A Formal Study of Myth*. Austin: University of Texas Press.
– (1968), *Kinship and Social Organization*. New York: Macmillan.
Burke, Kenneth (1966), *The Philosophy of Literary Form*. Berkeley: University of California Press.
Calloud, Jean (1976), *Structural Analysis of Narrative*. Philadelphia: Fortress Press.
– and François Genuty (1982), *La Première Épitre de Pierre: Analyse Semiotique*. Paris: Cerf.
Calvet, Louis J. (1973), *Roland Barthes*. Paris: Payot.
Carnap, Rudolf (1948), *Introduction to Semantics*. Cambridge: Harvard University Press.
Cassirer, Ernst (1953), *The Philosophy of Symbolic Forms*. I: *Language*. Translated by Ralph Mannheim. New Haven: Yale University Press.
– (1945), "Structuralism in Modern Lingustics." *Word* 1: 99-120.
Caws, Peter (1968), "What is Structuralism?" *Partisan Review* 35: 75-91
Charbonnier, G. (1969), ed. *Conversations with Claude Lévi-Strauss*. Translated by John Weightman and Doreen Weightman. London: Jonathan Cape.
Chatman, S. (1967), "The Semantics of Style." *Social Science Information* 6: 77-100.
Cherry, C. (1957), *On Human Communication*. Cambridge: M.I.T. Press.
Chomsky, Noam (1965), *Aspects of the Theory of Syntax*. Cambridge: M.I.T. Press.
– (1964), *Current Issues in Linguistic Theory*. The Hague: Mouton.
– (1968), *Language and Mind*. New York: Harcourt, Brace & World.
– (1957), *Syntactic Structures*. The Hague: Mouton.
– (1966), *Topics in the Theory of Generative Grammar*. The Hague: Mouton.
– and Halle, M. (1968), *The Sound Pattern in English*. New York: Harper & Row.
Clarke, Simon (1981), *The Foundations of Structuralism*. Brighton: The Harvester Press.
Colby, N. (1966), "Ethnographic Semantics." *Current Anthropology* 7: 3-32.
Corvez, M. (1969), *Les Structuralistes, les linguistes, les critiques littéraires: Michel Foucault, Claude Lévi-Strauss, Jacques Lacan, Louis Althusser*. Paris: Aubier-Montaigne.
Crespy, Georges (1973), "De la structure à l'analyse structurale." *Études Théologiques et Religieuses* 48: 11-34.
– (1973), "La parabole dite: 'Le bon Samaritain.' Recherches structurales." *Études Théologiques et Religieuses* 48: 61-79.
– (1966), "Psychanalyse et foi, analyse de la parabole de l'enfant prodigue." *Études Théologiques et Religieuses* 41: 241-51.
Crossan, J.D. (1973), *In Parables*. New York: Harper & Row.
– (1983), "It is Written: A Structuralist Analysis of John 6," *Semeia* 26: 3-21.
– (1973), "Parable and Example in the Teaching of Jesus." *New Testament Studies* 18: 285-307.
– (1973), "Structuralist Analysis and the Parables of Jesus." *Linguistica Biblica*, 41-51.
Culler, Johathan (1976), "Beyond Interpretation: The Prospects of Contemporary Criticism." *Comparative Literature*, 28.
– (1975), *Structuralist Poetics*. Ithaca, New York: Cornell University Press.
Culley, Robert (1976), *Studies in the Structure of Hebrew Narrative*. Philadelphia: Fortress Press.
Dearing, Vinton A. (1974), *Principles and Practice of Textual Analysis*. Berkeley: University of California Press.
Delorme, J. (1972), "Luc V. 1-11: Analyse Structurale et Histoire de la Rédaction." *New Testament Studies* 18: 331-50.
– (1972), "La resurrection dans le langage du NT." In *Le langage de foi dans l'Ecriture et dans le monde actuel*, pp. 101-82. Paris: Cerf.
Derrida, J. (1967), *l'Ecriture et la différence*. Paris: Editions du Seuil.

– (1976), *Of Grammatology*. Baltimore: Jons Hopkins University Press.
– (1977), "Signature, Event, Context." In *Glyphi I*. pp. 172-97. Baltimore: Johns Hopkins University Press.
Dixon, R.M.W. (1964), "On Formal and Contextual Meaning." *Acta Linguistica Academiae Scientiarum Hungaricae* 14: 23-46.
Donato, Eugenio (1967), "Of Structuralism and Literature." *Modern Language Notes* 82: 549-74.
Ducrot, Oswald; Todorov, T.; Sperber, D.; Safouan, M.; and Wald, F. (1968), *Qu'est-ce que le structuralisme?* Paris: Editions du Seuil.
Dulles, A. (1966), "Symbol, Myth and the Biblical Revelation." *Theological Studies* 27: 1-26.
Dumas, Andre (1973), "Décodage personnel." *Études Théologiques et Religieuses* 48: 3-6.
Dupont, L.; Lash, C.; and Levesque, G. (1973), "Recherche sur la structure de Jean 20." *Biblica* 54: 482-98.
Durkheim, E. (1965), *The Elementary Forms of Religious Life*. Translated by J.W. Swain. New York: Free Press.
– (1963), *Incest: The Nature and Origin of the Taboo*. Translated by Edward Sagarin. New York: Lyle Stuart.
– and Mauss Marcel (1963), *Primitive Classifications*. Translated by Rodney Needham. Chicago: University of Chicago Press.
Ebeling, G. (1950), "Die Bedeutung der historisch-kritischen Methode für die protestantische Theologie und Kirche." *Zeitschrift fur Theologie und Kirche* 47: 1-46 (reprinted in G. Ebeling. *Word and Faith* I: pp. 17-61. Translated by J.W. Leitch. Philadelphia: Fortress Press, 1963).
Ebeling, L. (1960), *Linguistic Units*. The Hague: Mouton.
Eco, Umberto (1971), *Le forme del contenuto*. Milan: Bompiani.
– (1976), *A Theory of Semiotics*. Bloomington: Indiana University Press.
Erlich, V. (1955), *Russian Formalism*. The Hague: Mouton.
Esbroeck, M. Van (1968), *Herméneutique, structuralisme et exégèse*. Paris: Desclee.
Fabian, Johannes (1971), "Language, History, and a New Anthropology." *Journal for the Philosophy of the Social Sciences* 1:19-47.
Finley, M.I. (1965), "Myth, Memory and History." *History and Theory* 4: 281-302.
Fischer, J.L. (1963), "The Sociopsychological Analysis of Folktales." *Current Anthropology* 4: 235-95.
Fodor, J.A. and Katz, J.J. (1964), ed. *The Structure of Language: Readings in the Philosophy of Language*. Englewood Cliffs, New Jersey: Prentice Hall.
Foucalt, Michel (1970), *The Order of Things*. New York: Random House.
Freedman, Ralph (1967), "Symbol as Terminus: Some Notes on Symbolist Narrative." *Comparative Literature Studies* 4:135-43.
Freedman, Sanford and Carole Taylor (1983), *Roland Barthes: A Bibliographical Reader's Guide*. New York: Garland.
Funk, R.W. (1967), "The Form and Structure of II and III John." *Journal of Biblical Literature* 86: 424-30.
Gaboury, A. (1970), *La structure des evangiles synoptiques. La structure-type à l'origine des synoptiques*. Supplements to *Novum Testamentum* 22. Leiden: E.J. Brill.
Gadamer, Hans-Georg (1975), *Truth and Method*. New York: Seabury Press.
Galland, Corina (1973), "Introduction à Greimas." *Études Théologiques et Religieuses* 48: 35-48.
Geertz, Clifford (1967), "The Cerebral Savage: On the Work of Claude Lévi-Strauss." *Encounter* 28: 25-32.
Genette, G. (1976), "Formalisme et langage poétique." *Comparative Literature* 28: 233-42.

– (1956), "Structuralisme et critique littéraire." *l'Arc* 26.
Gewalt, D. (1972), "'Formgeschichtliche' und/oder 'linguistische' Exegese?" *Linguistica Biblica* 19: 28-30.
Giavini, G. (1970), "La Structure Littéraire d'Eph. II. 11-22." *New Testament Studies* 16: 209-11.
Goddard, David (1965), "Conceptions of Structure in Lévi-Strauss and in British Anthropology." *Social Research* 32: 408-27.
Greenwood, David (1971), *The Nature of Science*. New York: Kennikat Press.
– (1970), "Rhetorical Criticism and Formgeschichte: Some Methodological Considerations." *Journal of Biblical Literature* 89: 418-26.
– (1957), *Truth and Meaning*. New York: Philosophical Library.
Greig, J.C.G. (1971), "Some Aspects of Hermeneutics: A Brief Survey." *Religion* 1: 131-51.
Greimas, Algirdas Julien (1970), *Du sens*. Paris: Editions du Seuil.
– (1983), *Du sens II*. Paris: Editions du Seuil.
– (1966), *Sémantique structurale*. Paris: Larousse.
– and J. Courtés. (1983), *Semiotics and Language: An Analytical Dictionary*. Bloomington: Indiana University Press.
– Et Al. (1970), *Sign, Language, Culture*. The Hague: Mouton.
Güttgemanns, E. (1968), "Christos in I Kor. 15, 3b – Titel oder Eigenname?" *Evangelische Theologie* 28: 533-54.
– (1973), "Einleitende Bemerkungen zur strukturalen Erzählforschung." *Linguistica Biblica* 23-24: 2-47.
– (1966), *Der leidende Apostel und sein Herr. Studien zur paulinischen Christologie*. Göttingen: Vandenhoech & Ruprecht.
– (1972), "Linguistische Analyse von Mk 16, 1-8." *Linguistica Biblica* 11-12: 13-53.
– (1972), "Linguistisch-literaturwissenschaftliche Grundlegung einer Neutestamentlichen Theologie." *Linguistica Biblica* 13-14: 2-18.
– (1970), "Literatur zur Neutestamentlichen Theologie: Überblick über Fortgang und Ziele der Forschung." *Verkündigung und Forschung* 15: 41-75.
– (1973), "Narrative Analyse synoptischer Texte." *Linguistica Biblica* 25-26: 50-73.
– (1971), *Offene Fragen zur Formgeschichte des Evangeliums: eine methodologische Skizze der Grundlagenproblematik der Form- und Redaktionsgeschichte*. Munich: Kaiser.
– (1972), "Qu'est-ce que la Poétique Générative? Thèses et réflexions pour la discussion des recherches concertées a Lyon-Fourvière (4-5-6 juillet 1972) 'Langage theologique et sciences du langage.'" *Linguistica Biblica* 19: 2-12.
– (1973), "Die synoptische Frage im Licht der modernen Sprach-und Literaturwissenschaft I." *Linguistica Biblica* 29-30: 2-40.
– (1972), "'Text' und 'Geschichte' als Grundkategorien der Generativen Poetik. Thesen zur aktullen Diskussion um die 'Wirklichkeit' der Auferstehungstexte." *Linguistica Biblica* 11-12: 2-12.
Gumperz, J.J. and Hymes, D. (1972), *Directions in Sociolinguistics*. New York: Holt, Rinehart & Winston.
Gunkel, H. (1964), *Genesis: Handkommentar zum Alten Testament*. Göttingen: Vandenhoeck & Ruprecht.
Halle, Morris (1956), ed. *For Roman Jakobson on the Occasion of His Sixtieth Birthday*. The Hague: Mouton.
Harari, F. and Ross, I.C. (1954), "The Number of Complete Cycles in a Communication Network." *Journal of Social Psychology* 40: 329-32.
Harris, Marvin (1968), *The Rise of Anthropological Theory: A History of Theories of Culture*. New York: T.Y. Crowell, (see especially his chapter on "French Structuralism").

Harris, A.S. (1951), *Methods in Structural Linguistics*. Chicago: University of Chicago Press.

Hawkes, Terence (1977), *Structuralism and Semiotics*. Berkeley: University of California Press.

Heller, L.G. and Maris, James (1970), *Toward a Structural Theory of Literary Analysis*. Worcester, Mass.: Institute of Systems Analysis.

Herndon, Jeanne (1976), *A Survey of Modern Grammars*. New York: Holt, Rinehart & Winston.

Hick, John (1977), ed. *The Myth of God Incarnate*. Philadelphia: Westminster Press.

Hirsch, E.D. (1976), *The Aims of Interpretation*. Chicago: University of Chicago Press.

Hjelmslev, Louis (1963), *Prolegomena to a Theory of Language*. Translated by F.J. Whitfield. Madison: University of Wisconsin Press.

Hoijer, H. (1963), ed. *Language in Culture*. Chicago: University of Chicago Press.

Hough, Graham (1977), "The Importation of Roland Barthes." *The Times Literary Supplement* 3950: 1443.

Hull, W.E. (1967), "A Structural Analysis of the Gospel of Luke." *Review and Expositor* 64: 421-25.

Hymes, D. (1968), "The Ethnography of Speaking." In *Readings in the Sociology of Language*. Edited by Joshua A. Fischman. The Hague: Mouton.

– (1964), ed. *Language in Culture and Society*. New York: Harper & Row.

International Encyclopedia of the Social Sciences, 1968. S.v. "The Comparative Method in Anthropology." by E.R. Leach.

International Encyclopedia of Unified Sciences, 1938. S.v. "Foundations of a Theory of Signs," by C.W. Morris.

Jackson, Jared and Kessler, Martin (1974), *Rhetorical Criticism*. Pittsburgh: Pickwick Press.

Jacob, A. (1969), "Sur le Structuralisme." *Etudes Philosophiques* 2: 173-86.

Jakobson, Roman (1960), "Concluding Statement: Linguistics and Poetics." In *Style in Language*, pp. 350-77. Edited by Thomas A. Sebeok. Cambridge: M.I.T. Press.

– (1966), *Poetics*. II: *Problems of General Metrics and the Metrics of Slavonic Languages*. The Hague: Mouton.

– (1971), *Selected Writings*. 2nd ed. 6 vols. The Hague: Mouton.

– and Halle, M. (1971), *Fundamentals of Language*. 2nd ed. The Hague: Mouton.

– and Tynyanov, J. (1966), "Problems of Literary and Linguistic Studies. *New Left Review* 37: 59-61.

– Gunnar, C.; Fant, M.; and Halle, M. (1961), *Preliminaries to Speech Analysis: The Distinctive Features and Their Correlates*. Cambridge: M.I.T. Press.

Jameson, Fredric (1972), *The Prison-House of Language: A Critical Account of Structuralism and Russian Formalism*. Princeton: Princeton University Press.

Johnson, Alfred M. (1976), ed. and translator. *The New Testament and Structuralism*. Pittsburgh: Pickwick Press. This work contains a valuable Glossary of Formalist and Structuralist Terms (pp. 251-322): it was the first of its kind to be compiled.

– (1976), ed. and translator. *Structural Analysis and Biblical Exegesis*. Pittsburgh: Pickwick Press.

– (1980), translator. *The Semiotics of the Passion Narrative: Topics and Figures*. Pittsburgh: Pickwick Press. (French version, see Louis Marin.)

Josselin De Jong, J.P. (1952), *Lévi-Strauss' Theory on Kinship and Marriage*. Leiden: E.J. Brill.

Kaufman, Gordon (1975), *An Essay on Theological Method*. Missoula, Montana: Scholars Press.

Kessler, M. (1971), "New Directions in Biblical Exegesis." *Scottish Journal of Theology* 24: 317-25.

Kirk, G.S. (1971), *Myth: Its Meaning and Functions in Ancient and Other Cultures.* Berkeley: University of California Press.

Klauck, H.J. (1972), "Neue Beiträge zur Gleichnisforschung." *Bibel und Leben* 13: 214-30.

Köbben, A.J.F. (1966), "Structuralism versus Comparative Functionalism." *Bijdragen Tot de Taal-, Land-, en Volkenkunde* 122: 145-50.

Köller, Wilhelm (1975), *Semiotik and Metapher.* Stuttgart: J.B. Metzler.

Köngäs, Elli-Kaija and Miranda, Pierre (1962), "Structural Models in Folklore." *Midwest Folklore* 12: 133-92.

Korn, F. (1969), "An Analysis of the Use of the Term 'Model' in some of Lévi-Strauss' Works." *Bijdragen Tot de Taal-, Land-, en Volkenkunde* 125: 1-11.

Kristeva, Julia (1975), "D'une identité l'autre." *Tel Quel* 62: 10-27.

Ladriere, J. (1970), *l'Articulation du Sens.* Paris: Desclée de Brouwer.

Lamarche, P. (1968), "Le Possédé de Gérasa (Mat. 8:28-34; Mc. 5:1-20; Luc. 8:26-39)." *Nouvelle Revue Théologique* 90: 581-97.

Lane, Michael (1970), *Introduction to Structuralism.* New York: Basic Books.

Langacker, Ronald (1973), *Language and Its Structure.* New York: Harcourt, Brace & Jovanovich.

Lanteri-Laura, G. (1967), "History and Structure in Anthropological Knowledge." *Social Research* 34: 115-61.

Laplanche, Jean and Pontalis, Jean (1973), *The Language of Psychoanalysis.* Translated by Donald Nicholson-Smith. London: Hogarth Press.

Lapointe, R. (1973), "Actualité de l'apocalyptique." *Eglise et Théologie* 4: 197-211.

– (1972), "Structuralisme et exégèse." *Science et Esprit* 24: 135-53.

– (1971), "La valeur linguistique du Sitz im Leben." *Biblica* 52: 469-87.

Lavers, Annette (1971), "Some Aspects of Language in the Work of Jacques Lacan." *Semiotica* 3: 269-79.

– (1982), translator. *Roland Barthes: Structuralism and After.* Cambridge, Mass.: Harvard University Press.

Leach, Edmund (1965), "Claude Lévi-Strauss: Anthropologist and Philosopher." *New Left Review* 34: 12-27 (also in R.A. Manners and D. Kaplan, ed. *Theory in Anthropology*, pp. 541-50. Chicago: Aldine, 1969).

– (1968), *Dialectic in Practical Religion.* Cambridge: Cambridge University Press.

– (1969), *Genesis as Myth: And Other Essays.* London: Jonathan Cape.

– (1966), "The Legitimacy of Solomon." *European Journal of Sociology* 7: 58-101.

– (1974), *Lévi-Strauss.* London: Fontana.

– (1965), "Review of *Mythologiques I: Le Cru et le cuit.*" *American Anthropologist* 67: 776-80.

– (1967), ed. *The Structural Study of Myth and Totemism.* London: Tavistock.

– with D. Alan Aycock (1983), *Structuralist Interpretations of Biblical Myth.* Cambridge: Cambridge University Press.

Leeden, A.C. Van Der (1971), "'Empiricism' and 'Logical Order' in 'Anthropological Structuralism.'" *Bijdragen Tot de Taal-, Land-, en Volkenkunde* 127: 15-38.

Leenhardt, F.J. (1950), "La Parabole de Samaritain: Schema d'une exégèse existentialiste." In *Aux sources de la Tradition chretienne: Melanges offerts à M. Maurice Goguel à l'occasion de son soixantedixième anniversaire*, pp. 132-38. Neuchâtel: Delanchaux & Niestlé.

Lehman, A.G. (1950), *The Symbolist Aesthetic in France: 1885-1895.* Oxford: Basil Blackwell.

Lemon, Lee T. and Reis, Marian J. (1965), ed. and translator. *Russian Formalist Criticism: Four Essays.* Lindoln: University of Nebraska Press.

Leon-Dufour, X. (1970), "Exégètes et Structuralistes." *Recherches de Science Religieuse* 58: 5-15.

Lesage, L. (1967), *The New French Criticism.* University Park: Pennsylvania State University Press.

Lessa, William A. and Vogt, Evon Z. (1972), ed. *Reader in Comparative Religion: An Anthropological Approach.* 3rd ed. New York: Harper & Row.

Lévi-Strauss, Claude (1960), "l'Analyse morphologiques des contes russes." *International Journal of Slavic Linguistics and Poetics* 3: 122-49.

– (1958), *Anthropologie structurale.* Paris: Plon. (English version: *Structural Anthropology.* New York: Basic Books, 1963).

– (1966), "Anthropology: Its Achievements and Future." *Current Anthropology* 7: 124-27.

– (1954), "The Art of Deciphering Symbols." *Diogenes* 5: 102-08.

– (1963), "The Bear and the Barber." *Journal of the Royal Anthropological Institute* 93: 1-11.

– (1960), "Ce que l'Ethnologie doit à Durkheim." *Annales de l'Université de Paris* 30: 47-50.

– (1961), "'Comment' to the 'Classification of Double Descent Systems' by J. Goody." *Current Anthropology* 2: 3-25.

– (1962), "Compte Rendu du Colloque sur le Mot 'Structure.'" In *Sens et Usages du Terme 'Structure' dans les Sciences Humaines et Sociales.* edited by R. Bastide. The Hague: Mouton.

– (1967), "A Contre-Courant." Interview with Claude Lévi-Strauss by G. Dumar. *Le Nouvel Observateur* 115: 30-2.

– (1966), "A Conversation with Claude Lévi-Strauss by G. Steiner." *Encounter* 36: 32-8.

– (1972), "A Conversation with Lévi-Strauss" by A. Akoun, F. Morin and J. Mousseau. *Psychology Today* 5: 37-9; 74-82.

– (1969), *Conversations with Claude Lévi-Strauss.* Edited by G. Charbonnier. London: Jonathan Cape.

– (1964), "Criteria of Science in the Social and Human Disciplines." *International Social Science Journal* 16: 534-52.

– (1969), *The Elementary Structures of Kinship.* Translated by James Harle Bell and John Richard von Sturmer. Edited by Rodney Needham. Boston: Beacon Press.

– (1971), "Interview with Lévi-Strauss." *l'Express* 15: 60-6.

– (1968), *Mythologiques: Le cru et le cuit.* Paris: Plon.

– (1954), "What is a Primitive?" *UNESCO Courier* 7: 5-7.

– (1984), *Le Regard éloigné.* Paris: Plon.

Levin, David Michael (1968), "On Lévi-Strauss and Existentialism." *American Scholar* 38: 69-82.

Levitt, Paul M. (1971), *A Structural Approach to the Analysis of Drama.* The Hague: Mouton.

Löwith, Karl (1949), *Meaning in History.* Chicago: University of Chicago Press.

Lounsbury, F.G. (1964), "The Structural Analysis of Kinship Semantics." In *Proceedings of the IXth International Congress of Linguistics.* Edited by H.G. Lunt. The Hague: Mouton.

Louw, J.P. (1973), "Discourse Analysis and the Greek New Testament." *Bible Translator* 24: 101-18.

Lyttkens, H. (1970), "Bibletolkningen och dess problem" [Bible Interpretation and Its Problems]. *Svensk Teologisk Kvartalskrift* 46: 97-110.

Macksey, Richard and Donato, Eugenio (1970), ed. *The Structuralist Controversy: The Language of Criticism and the Sciences of Man.* Baltimore: Johns Hopkins Press.

Magass, W. (1973), "Semiotik einer Tishordnung (Lk. 14: 7-14)." *Linguistica Biblica* 25-26: 2-8.

Magass, W. (1972), Zur Semiotik der signifikanten Orte in den Gleichnissen Jesu."
Linguistica Biblica 15-16: 3-21.
Malamat, A. (1967), "Comments on Edmund Leach: 'The Legitimacy of Solomon,'
Some Structural Aspects." *European Journal of Sociology* [Archives Européenes de
Sociologie 8: 165-67.
Maranda, Elli Et Al. (1971), *Structural Models in Folklore and Transformational Essays.*
The Hague: Mouton.
Maranda, P. (1972), ed. *Mythology.* London: Penguin Books.
– and Kongas, ed. (1971), ed. *Structural Analysis of Oral Tradition.* Philadelphia:
University of Pennsylvania Press.
Marin, Louis (1973), "Du Corps au texte." *Esprit* 423: 913-28.
– (1970), "Essai d'analyse structurale d'Actes 10:1-11, 18." *Recherches de Science
Religieuse* 58: 39-61.
– (1971), "Essai d'analyse structurale d'un récit-parabole: Matthieu 13:1-23." *Études
Théologiques et Religieuses* 46: 35-74.
– (1971), *Sémiotique de la Passion.* Paris: Aubier, Cerf. (English version, see Alfred M.
Johnson.)
Marle, R. (1967), *Introduction to Hermeneutics.* Translated by E. Froment and R.
Albrecht. New York: Herder & Herder.
Martinet, A. (1964), *Elements of General Linguistics.* Translated by Elisabeth Palmer.
London: Faber & Faber.
– (1962), *A Functional View of Language.* Oxford: Clarendon Press.
Masson, Charles (1961), "Le démoniaque de Gérasa (Marc. 5:1-20)." In *Vers les sources
d'eau vive. Études d'exégèse et de théologie du Nouveau Testament,* pp. 20-37.
Lausanne: Librairie Payot.
Matejka, Ladislav and Pomorska, Krystyna (1971), ed. *Readings in Russian Poetics:
Formalist and Structuralist Views.* Cambridge: M.I.T. Press.
Mayenowa, M.R. (1967), "Semiotics Today: Reflections on the 2nd International
Conference on Semiotics." *Social Science Information* 6: 59-64.
McKnight, Edgar (1978), *Meaning in Texts.* Philadelphia: Fortress Press.
Mellon, C. (1973), "La Parabole: Manière de parler, manière d'entendre [Mt. 13:1-53]."
Recherches de Science Religieuse 61: 49-63.
Menard, J. (1970), "La structure et la langue originale de l'Evangile de vérité." *Revue
des Sciences Religieuses* 44: 128-37.
Merleau-Ponty, M. (1962), *The Phenomenology of Perception.* Translated by C. Smith.
London: Routledge & Humanities Press.
– (1964), *The Primacy of Perception.* Edited by James M. Edie. Evanston: North-
western University Press.
– (1964), *Sense and Non-sense.* Translated by H.L. Dreyfus and P.A. Dreyfus.Evanston:
Northwestern University Press.
– (1964), *Signs.* Translated by Richard C. McCleary. Evanston:Northwestern University
Press.
Michelet, Jules (1954), *Michelet par lui-même: images et textes présentées par Roland
Barthes.* Paris: Editions du Seuil.
Miller, J.H. (1966), "The Geneva School." *Critical Quarterly* 8: 305-21.
Milne, Pamela and Flanagan, James (1976), "Dialogue on Structuralism and Biblical
Studies." *Horizons* 3: 95-9.
Morris, C.W. (1964), *Signification and Significance: A Study of the Relations of Signs
and Values.* Cambridge: M.I.T. Press.
– (1946), *Signs, Language and Behavior.* Englewood Cliffs, New Jersey: Prentice-Hall.
Morris, Wesley (1979), *Friday's Footprint: Structuralism and the Articulated Text.*
Ohio: Ohio State University Press.

Mounin, G. (1968), *Saussure ou le Structuraliste sans le Savior.* Paris: Seghers.

Nathhorst, Bertel (1969), *Formal or Structural Studies of Traditional Tales: The Usefulness of Some Methodological Proposals Advanced by Valdimir Propp, Alan Dundes, Claude Lévi-Strauss, and Edmund Leach.* Stockholm: Amqvist & Wiksell.

Needham, Rodney (1962), *Structure and Sentiment: A Test Case in Social Anthropology.* Chicago: University of Chicago Press.

Nettl, Peter (1966), "Lévi-Strauss." *New Statesman* 72: 880-81.

Nutini, Hugh G. (1970), "A Comparison of Lévi-Strauss' Structuralism and Chomsky's Transformational Generative Grammar." In *Essays in Structural Anthropology: In Honor of Claude Lévi-Strauss.* Edited by Hugo G. Nutini and Ira R. Buchler. New York: Appleton-Century-Crofts.

— (1971), "The Ideological Bases of Lévi-Strauss' Structuralism." *American Anthropologist* 73: 537-44.

— (1970), "Lévi-Strauss' Conception of Science." In *Exchanges et Communications,* I: 543-70. Edited by J. Pouillon and P. Maranda. The Hague: Mouton.

— (1971), "Science and Ideology." *Bijdragen Tot de Taal-, Land-, en Volkenkunde* 127: 1-14.

— (1965), "Some Considerations on the Nature of Social Structure and Model Building: A Critique of Claude Lévi-Strauss and Edmund Leach." *American Anthropologist* 67: 707-31.

Ogden, C.K. and Richards, I.A. (1960), *The Meaning of Meaning.* London: Routledge & Kegan Paul.

Ong, Walter (1982), *Orality and Literacy.* London: Methuen.

Paper, Herbert (1975), ed. *Language and Texts.* Ann Arbor, Michigan: Center for Coordination of Ancient and Modern Studies.

Parin-Vial, J. (1969), *Analyses Structurales et idéologies structuralists.* Toulouse: Privat.

Patte, Daniel (1976), *Semiology and Parables.* Pittsburgh: Pickwick Press.

— (1975), "Structural Network in Narrative: The Good Samaritan." *Soundings* 58: 221-42.

— (1976), *What Is Structural Analysis?* Philadelphia: Fortress Press.

— and Patte, Aline (1978), *Structural Exegesis: From Theory to Practice.* Philadelphia: Fortress Press.

Paz, Octavio (1970), *Claude Lévi-Strauss: An Introduction.* Ithaca: Cornell University Press.

Perrin, N. (1972), "The Evangelist as Author: Reflections on Method in the Study and Interpretation of the Synoptic Gospels and Acts." *Biblical Research* 17: 5-18.

— (1967), "The Parables of Jesus as Parables, as Metaphors, and as Aesthetic Objects: A Review Article." *Journal of Religion* 47: 340-46.

Pesch, R. (1971), "Structures du ministère dans le Nouveau Testament." *Istina* 16: 437-52.

Pettit, Philip (1975), *The Conception of Structuralism: A Critical Analysis.* Berkeley: University of California Press.

Piaget, J. (1969), "Le Structuralisme." *Cahiers Internationaux de Symbolisme* 17-18: 73-85.

Picard, Raymond (1963), "Critical Trends in France." *Times Literary Supplement* 3213: 719-20.

Polzin, Robert (1977), *Biblical Structuralism.* Philadelphia: Fortress Press.

Pomorska, Krystyna (1968), *Russian Formalist Theory and Its Poetic Ambiance.* The Hague: Mouton.

Poole, R.C. (1966), "Indirect Communication. 2. Merleau-Ponty and Lévi-Strauss." *New Blackfriars* 47: 594-604.

Postal, Paul M. (1964), "Underlying and Superficial Linguistic Structure." *Harvard Educational Review* 34: 246-66.

Pouillon, J. (1956), "l'Oeuvre de Claude Lévi-Strauss." *Les Temps Modernes* 12.
– (1965), "Sartre et Lévi-Strauss." *l'Arc* 26: 55-60.
– (1966), "(Structuralisme) Présentation: un essai de définition." *Les Temps Modernes*
   22: 769-90.
– and Maranda, P. (1970), ed. *Exchanges et Communications*. The Hague: Mouton.
Propp, Vladimir (1968), *The Morphology of the Folktale*. 2nd ed. Translated by Lau-
   rence Scott. Edited by Louis Wagner. Austin: University of Texas Press.
Radcliff-Brown, A.R. (1952), *Structure and Function in Primitive Society*. New York:
   Free Press.
Ramaroson, L. (1974), "La structure du premier Evangile." *Science et Esprit* 26:69-112.
Reese, J.M. (1972), "Literary Structure of Jn 13:31-14:31; 16:5-6; 16-33." *Catholic
   Biblical Quarterly* 34: 321-31.
Ricoeur, Paul (1965), *History and Truth*. Translated by Charles A. Kelbley. Evanston:
   Northwestern University Press.
– *Les Incidences Théologiques des recherches actuelles concernant le langage*. Paris:
   Institut d'Etudes Oecuméniques, (n.d.).
– (1963), "Structure et herméneutique." *Esprit* 31: 596-627.
– (1967), "La Structure, le mot, l'evénement." *Esprit* 35: 801-21.
Rifflet-Lemaire, Anika (1970), *Jacques Lacan*. Brussels: Dessart.
Ringgren, H. (1960), "Literarkritik, Formgeschichte, Überlieferungsgeschichte." *Theo-
   logische Literaturzeitung* 91: 641-50.
Riesenfeld, H. (1961), "Symboliken som uttrycksmedel i evangelierna" [Symbolism as
   a Means of Expression in the Gospels]. *Svensk Exegetisk Arsbok* 26: 42-56.
Robinson, D.W.B. (1972), "The Literary Structure of Hebrews 1:1-4." *Australian
   Journal of Biblical Archaeology* 2: 178-86.
Rogerson, J. (1970), "Structural Anthropology and the Old Testament." *Bulletin of
   the School of Oriental and African Studies* 33: 490-500.
Rossi, Ino (1973), "Reply to Nutini's 'The Ideological Bases of Lévi-Strauss." *American
   Anthropologist* 75: 20-48.
Rue, L.O. (1973), "Michael Polanyi and the Critical Approach to Sacred Texts." *Dialog*
   12: 117-20.
Sartre, Jean-Paul (1971), "Replies to Structuralism." *Telos* 6: 110-16.
– (1968), *Search for a Method*. Translated by Hazel E. Barnes. New York: Vintage
   Press.
Saussure, Ferdinand De (1966), *Course in General Linguistics*. Translated by Wade
   Baskin. Edited by Charles Bally and Albert Sechehaye. New York: McGraw-Hill.
Scheflen, A.E. (1967), "Psychoanalytic Terms and Some Problems of Semiotics."
   Social Science Information 6: 113-22.
Schiwy, G. (1971), Neue Aspekte des Strukturalismus. Munich: Kösel-Verlag.
– (1971), *Structuralism and Christianity*. Translated by Henry J. Koren. Pittsburgh:
   Duquesne University.
– (1973), *Strukturalismus und Zeichensysteme*. Munich: Beck.
Schnackenburg, Rudolf (1973), "Strukturanalyse von Joh 17." *Biblische Zeitschrift*
   17: 67-78; 196-202.
Schneider, D.M. (1965), "Some Muddles in the Models: Or How the System Really
   Works." In *The Relevance of Models for Social Anthropology*, pp. 25-85. Edited by
   M. Banton. New York: Praeger. (London: Tavistock, 1968, pp. 25-85).
Schneider, F. and Stenger, W. (1972), "Beobachtungen zur Struktur der Emmausperi-
   kope (Lk. 24:13-35)." *Biblische Zeitschrift* 16: 94-114.
Scholes, Robert (1974), *Structuralism in Literature: An Introduction*. New Haven: Yale
   University Press.
Seung, T.K. (1982), *Structuralism and Hermeneutics*. New York: Columbia University
   Press.

Scott, Bernard (1981), *Jesus, Symbol-Maker for the Kingdom.* Philadelphia: Fortress Press.

Sommerfelt, A. (1965), "Linguistic Structures and the Structures of Social Groups." *Diogenes* 51: 186-92.

Spiegel, Yorick (1972), ed. *Psychoanalytische Interpretationen biblisher Texte.* Munich: Kaiser Verlag.

Starobinsky, Jean (1971), "An Essay in Literary Analysis – Mark 5:1-20." *The Ecumenical Review* 23: 377-97.

– (1973), "The Struggle with Legion: A Literary Analysis of Mark 5:1-20." *New Literary History* 6: 331-56.

Stokoe, W.C. (1972), *Semiotics and Human Sign Language.* New York: Humanities Press.

Sturrock, John (1979), ed. *Structuralism and Since.* Oxford: Oxford University Press.

Strelka, Joseph (1968), ed. *Perspectives in Literary Symbolism.* University Park: Pennsylvania State University Press.

Taber, C.R. (1969), "Exegesis and Linguistics." *Bible Translator* 20: 150-53.

Thiselton, A.C. (1973), "The Use of Philosophical Categories in New Testament Hermeneutics." *Churchman* 87: 87-100.

Thody, Philip (1977), *Roland Barthes.* London: Macmillan.

Thurley, Geoffrey (1983), *Counter-Modernism in Current Critical Theory.* London: Macmillan.

Tiryakian, Edward A. (1965), "Existential Phenomenology and the Sociological Tradition." *American Sociological Review* 30: 674-88.

Topel, L.J. (1971), "A Note on the Methodology of Structural Analysis in Jn. 2:23-3:21." *Catholic Biblical Quarterly* 33: 211-20.

Troubetzkoy, N. (1969), *Principles of Phonology.* Berkeley: University of California Press.

Turnell, M. (1966), "Criticism of Roland Barthes." *Encounter* 26: 30-6.

Turner, Victor W. (1969), *The Ritual Process: Structure and Anti-Structure.* Chicago: Aldine.

Vachek, J. (1964), ed. *A Prague School Reader in Linguistics.* Bloomington: Indiana University Press.

Vanhoye, A. (1963), *La structure littéraire de l'épitre aux Hébreux.* Paris: Desclée de Brouwer.

Via, Dan O., Jr. (1961), "Darkness: Christ and the Church in the Fourth Gospel." *Scottish Journal of Theology* 14: 172-93.

– (1975), *Kerygma and Comedy in the New Testament: A Structuralist Approach to Hermeneutic.* Philadelphia: Fortress Press.

– (1973), "Parable and Example Story: A Literary-structuralist Approach." *Linguistica Biblica* 25-26: 21-30.

– (1971), "The Relationship of Form to Content in the Parables: The Wedding Feast [Matt. 22:1-10]." *Interpretation* 25: 171-84.

– (1974), A Structuralist Approach to Paul's Old Testament Hermeneutic." *Interpretation* 28: 201-20.

Vilar, P. (1962), "La notion de structure en historie." In *Sens et usage du terme "structure" dans les sciences humaines.* The Hague: Mouton.

Wald, Henri (1969), "Structure, Structural, Structuralism." *Diogenes* 66: 15-24.

Wetherill, P.M. (1974), *The Literary Text: An Examination of Critical Methods.* Berkeley: University of California Press.

Wilden, Anthony (1972), *System and Structure: Essays in Communication and Exchange.* London: Tavistock.

– (1972), "Structuralism, Communication, Evolution." *Semiotica* 6:244-56.

Wilder, Amos (1976), *Theopoetic*. Philadelphia: Fortress Press.
Zaklad, J. (1971), "Création, péché originel et formalisme (Gen. I-III)." *Revue d'Histoire et de Philosophie Religieuses* 51: 1-30.

II: Journal Issues

Annales: Economie Societies Civilisations. Paris. Vol. 19, No. 6 (November-December 1964).
L'arc (Aix-en-Provence). No. 26, 1965.
Communications. Paris. No. 4, 1964; No. 8, 1966.
L'Esprit. Paris. No. 322. November 1963.
Études Théologiques et Religieuses. Vol. 48, No. 1. Montpellier, France, 1973.
Human Context. The Hague. Vol. 5, No. 1, 1973.
International Journal of Sociology. Vol. 2, Nos. 2-3, 1972.
Interpretation. Richmond, Va. Vol. 28, Spring 1974.
Langages. Paris. No. 22, June, 1971.
Language Sciences. Indiana University. No. 17, October 1971.
Recherches de Science Religieuse. Paris. Vol. 58, No. 1, 1970.
Revue Internationale de Philosophie. Brussels. Nos. 73-74, 1965.
Revue des Sciences Philosophiques et Théologiques. Paris. No. 49, October 1965.
Semeia. Missoula, Montana. Nos. 1, 2 (1974); 6 (1976); 16, 18 (1980); 19 (1981); 23 (1982) 26, 29 (1983).
Social Compass. The Hague. Vol. 20, No. 3, 1973.
Social Science Information. Paris. Vol. 6, Nos. 2-4, 1967.
Sociologie et Sociétés. Montréal. Vol. 5, No. 2, 1973.
Soundings. Nashville, Tennessee. Vol. 58, No. 2, 1975.
Les Temps Modernes. Paris. No. 246, November 1966.
Yale French Studies. New Haven: Conn. Nos. 36-37, October 1966. (These issues have been reprinted as a monograph: J. Ehrmann, ed., *Strucuralism*. New York: Double-Day, 1970.)

Index

Actant, Greimas's definition, 9, 55-6, 65-6, 80; Güttgemann's use, 79; actantial model (Marin), 97-8; semantized, 132

Aristotle, 77; reformulation of the concepts in the *Poetics* (Güttgemanns), 77-8; Square of Opposition, 34-5

Bach, Emmon, 112, 121n

Barbut, Marc, 5

Barthes, Roland, 3, 9, 63; *Analyse Structurale et Exégèse Biblique:* 42, 58-60; on codes in general, 4, 44-5; comparison with Gunkel's approach, 48-52; on *écriture,* 10; *Elements of Semiology,* 10, 41; Influence of Marx and Freud on, 10, 41, 43, 54, 59; on meaning, 52-3; as structuralist, 41; on structuralist procedure, 47; on the text, 44-5; use of Propp's functions, 56-8; writing as desire, 43, 60n, 61n, 91, 93, 96, 104, 114, 117, 121n, 123

Benveniste, Emile, 6

Bible: account of Creation as anti-myth in the, 20; achronic approach to the, 15; Barthes's treatment of Genesis 32: 22-32, 42, 46, 48-60; (contrasted to Gunkel's), 51-2; Calloud's analysis of the temptation story in Matthew 4: 1-11, 68-9; Chabrol's *"Analyse du 'Texte' de la Passion,"* 91-2; as complex network of structures, 8, 11; disadvantages of Propp's method for biblical studies, 108-9; Galatians I: 1-10, paradigmatic and syntagmatic readings of, 24-5; *Genesis,* purpose of writers in, 19, 21; Marin's *"Sémiotique de la Passion,* 97-101; the Ordeal of Isaac: Genesis 22: 1-19, 123-24; (analysis of), 124-29; the Parable of the Good Samaritan: Patte's analysis and previous controversy, 26-32, 37; the Prodigal Son: Luke 15: 11-32, 129-30;

(analysis of), 130-38; Starobinski's "The Struggle with Legion: A Literary Analysis of Mark 5:1-20," 92-6; Structuralist Analysis of the Creation Myth, 16-7; Structuralist methods for biblical texts, 3, 7, 9, 94; Translations, 20, 138n

Binarism (binary oppositions), 16; in Greimas, 64; in mythical systems, 17

Blanché, Robert: on the validity of the semiotic square, 36

Bloomfield, Leonard, 2

Boas, Franz, 2

Boudon, Raymond, 112, 121n

Bremond, Claude, 67, 72n, 111; criticism of Greimas's method, 68

Bultmann, Rudolf, 39n, 77, 82, 84-6, 111

Calloud, Jean, 63, 68, 72n, 73n; analysis of the temptation story in Matthew 4: 1-11, 68-9; strengths and weaknesses in his analysis, 70-1

Camus, Albert, 10

Carnap, R., 7

Caws, Peter, 12n

Chabrol, Claude: *"Analyse du 'Texte' de la Passion,"* 91-2, 105n; criticism of his methodology, 92

Chomsky, Noam, 4, 5, 7, 30-1, 75, 85, 88n, 89n

Classeme, 65

Code, 4; Barthes's codes of narration, 44-5

Comedy, 78, 101-2

Competence: as a concept in linguistics and poetics, 13-14, 64, 75, 81, 88n

Cornford, Francis, 101-2; 106n

Crossan, J. D., Derrida's influence on, 120; on the Good Samaritan, 26-7; on parable Vs example story, 27-9; 121n

Culler, Jonathan, on structuralists and post-structuralists, 119, 121n

Derrida, Jacques: on *écriture,* 120; 121n

de Saussure. *See* Saussure